CROSSROADS

Commandments

Author
Richard J. Reichert

BROWN-ROA
A Division of Harcourt Brace & Company

Our Mission

The primary mission of BROWN-ROA is to provide the Catholic and Christian educational markets with the highest quality catechetical print and media resources. The content of these resources reflects the best insights of current theology, methodology, and pedagogical research. The resources are practical and easy to use, designed to meet expressed market needs, and written to reflect the teachings of the Catholic Church.

Nihil Obstat
Rev. Richard L. Schaefer
Imprimatur
✠ Most Rev. Jerome Hanus, O.S.B.
Archbishop of Dubuque
January 4, 1998
Feast of Saint Elizabeth Ann Seton

The Imprimatur is an official declaration that a book or pamphlet is free of doctrinal or moral error. No implication is contained therein that anyone who granted the Imprimatur agrees with the contents, opinions, or statements expressed.

Copyright © 1999 by BROWN-ROA, a division of Harcourt Brace & Company

All rights reserved. No part of this publication may be reproduced or transmitted in any form or by any means, electronic or mechanical, including photocopy, recording, or any information storage and retrieval system, without permission in writing from the publisher.

Requests for permission to make copies of any part of the work should be mailed to the following address: Permissions Department, Harcourt Brace & Company, 6277 Sea Harbor Drive, Orlando, Florida 32887-6777.

Portions of this work were published in previous editions.

The Scripture quotations contained herein are from the New Revised Standard Version Bible: Catholic Edition copyright © 1993 and 1989 by the Division of Christian Education of the National Council of the Churches of Christ in the U.S.A. Used by permission. All rights reserved.

Excerpts from the English translation of the *Catechism of the Catholic Church* for use in the United States of America Copyright © 1994, United States Catholic Conference, Inc.—Libreria Editrice Vaticana. Used with Permission.

Illustrations: Rob Suggs

Photo Credits: Mimi Forsyth—58; James L. Shaffer—iv, 15, 17, 19, 23, 25, 41, 50, 54, 67, 76, 88, 93, 94; Skjold Photography—7, 31, 34, 38, 43, 49, 52, 56, 64, 69, 78, 83; D. Jeanene Tiner—2; Jim Whitmer—1

Printed in the United States of America

ISBN 0-15-950469-4

10 9 8 7 6 5 4

Contents

Chapter 1: Taking Command 1
- *Rules to live by*
- *Physical, moral, and divine laws*
- *The Greatest Commandment*

Chapter 2: I Am the Lord Your God 14
- *It's all about faith, hope, and charity*
- *Whom do you worhsip?*

Chapter 3: You Shall Not Take the Name of the Lord Your God in Vain/Remember to Keep Holy the Sabbath Day 26
- *It's all about respect*
- *A reminder of God's creation*
- *The Sunday Eucharist*

Chapter 4: Honor Your Father and Your Mother 38
- *God is our Father*
- *The Christian family*
- *Jesus gave honor to his Father*

Chapter 5: You Shall Not Kill 52
- *The gift of life*
- *The practice of nonviolence*
- *All life is sacred*

Chapter 6: You Shall Not Commit Adultery / You Shall Not Covet Your Neighbor's Wife 63
- *Love and faithfulness*
- *Developing friendships*
- *To love, honor, and cherish*

Chapter 7: You Shall Not Steal/You Shall Not Covet Your Neighbor's Goods 73
- *Respect for others*
- *Stewards of the earth*
- *Social justice*

Chapter 8: You Shall Not Bear False Witness 88
- *The source of all truth*
- *Called to bear witness*
- *The Golden Rule*

Appendix I: Glossary of Terms 98

Appendix II: Your Catholic Heritage 100

Chapter 1
Taking Command

A "TOP TEN" LIST OF RULES FOR LIFE

Create a "top ten" list of statements describing rules or guidelines you follow in your own life. Make sure to list your rules in the order of importance for your life.

1.
2.
3.
4.
5.
6.
7.
8.
9.
10.

Rules to live by

Wherever you go, it seems that someone is always telling you to "Do this" or "Don't do that." There are rules for everything, whether you're at home, at school, at the swimming pool, or at the movies.

There are rules about where you can skateboard or ride your bike, even when and where you can walk and talk. Are all these rules necessary? Some rules probably aren't necessary, but we do need some rules just to survive.

 ## A CONTINUING SAGA... (PART 1)

You are shipwrecked on a deserted island in the Pacific Ocean. You're all alone. On your island is one small spring where you can get water. There is one date palm tree that can supply you enough fruit to stay alive. There are also a few wild pigs and goats. You have a knife and an ax so you can make a shelter, a bow and a few arrows, and a fishing spear.

Since you are all alone, you're in charge. You can make all the rules. But do you need any rules? Actually, if you want to stay alive, you'll have to make a few rules for yourself.

What rules do you need to establish for yourself?

_____
_____
_____
_____

But now, after surviving on this deserted island alone for eight months, you notice someone floating to shore on a raft....

SOME "DO"S AND "DONT"S

Below are listed some places where certain rules are enforced. For each place, list a rule that people must follow and the reason for the rule. Then decide whether or not the rule is necessary and why you think that way. For example, lifeguards at the swimming pool are responsible for enforcing the rule that no running is allowed because people can slip on the water that has splashed on the floor. The rule is necessary because people may seriously hurt themselves if they fall.

Place	Rule enforced	Reason for the rule	Is the rule necessary?
School			
Home			
Movies			
Mall			
Park			
Other:			

In the following excerpt from his book, Pope John Paul II discusses the role of rules and hope in the youth of today.

If at every stage of his life man desires to be his own person, to find love, during his youth he desires it even more strongly. The desire to be one's own person, however, must not be understood as a license to do anything, without exception. The young do not want that at all—they are willing to be corrected, they want to be told yes or no. They need guides, and they want them close at hand. If they turn to authority figures, they do so because they see in them a wealth of human warmth and a willingness to walk with them along the paths they are following.

—Taken from Crossing the Threshold of Hope *by Pope John Paul II (New York: Knopf, 1994), page 121.*

At this stage in your life, you are becoming more and more familiar with what it means to "be your own person." You are learning what characteristics are a part of who you are, as well as which are not. Your parents and your teachers may be allowing you to make more and more of your own decisions. As you grow, it is beneficial to take stock in where you have been, where you are, and where you are going in regard to being your own person.

Journal

How do you feel about what Pope John Paul II says about willingness to be corrected, about wanting to be told yes or no? Think for a moment, then answer the following questions.

When was the last time you were corrected?
_____
_____

Who corrected you?
_____
_____

Why did the person correct you?
_____
_____

How did you respond to being corrected?
_____
_____

How did you feel?
_____
_____

What good came out of the situation?
_____
_____

I'D LIKE YOU TO MEET...

What is one way to learn more about someone, including yourself? Interviewing a person is a great way to learn more about a person. Look around the room and find someone whom you do not know very well. Pair up with this person and interview him or her about the person that he or she is becoming. The following points are some steps to help guide you in the interviewing process. Following the interview, you will be introducing your partner to the class, so you will want to know as much as you can about him or her.

1. Introduce yourself by shaking hands with your partner. Make sure to make eye contact with the person.
2. Establish some general background information (age, school, grade, family).
3. Discuss the person's decision-making process.
   - What are some decisions that you had to make five years ago?
   - What guided your decision-making process five years ago?
   - What decisions do you have to make now?
   - What guides your decision-making process now?
   - What decisions do you think you will have to make in the future?
   - What do you think will guide your decision-making process in the future?
4. Discuss what your partner likes best about himself or herself. Why does your partner think this is his or her best attribute?
5. Discuss what your partner likes least about himself or herself. Why does your partner think this is his or her worst attribute?

Carte blanche

Along with an increased understanding of who you are, you are now realizing that being free to be your own person does not mean that you are free to do whatever you want. Being your own person does not grant you *carte blanche*—the ability to do whatever you want with little or no regard for others. Part of being who you are involves being mindful and respectful of others.

Think back on the interview you just completed. How do you exhibit responsibility in your decisions? Which decisions involved other people? Did you take into consideration the thoughts and feelings of others? What does this say about you as a person?

Odds are that *some* good comes out of every situation. To help us see the good in everything, God gives us *guides* who help us become the best people that we can be. Right now, you have parents, teachers, coaches, and priests and other parish ministers who act as guides for you. As you get older, you will also have bosses, friends, and perhaps a spouse who will be willing to correct you and walk with you on the right path. They will help you make important decisions in your life.

In addition to these people, you also have other guides in your life, such as the Church. The Church gives us direction for our lives through the Ten Commandments, the law of love, the Beatitudes, the Golden Rule, and the teachings of the Church.

And as always, you can turn to the Holy Trinity for guidance. *Holy Trinity* is the name we give to the three Persons who are one God—the Father, the Son, and the Holy Spirit. The Trinity is the central mystery of our faith, containing this most basic truth, which we know through revelation: Sent by God the Father, Jesus Christ redeemed humankind by the power of the Holy Spirit.

God gives us grace to guide us. *Grace* is God's free gift of himself, the offer of God's love to humanity, which precedes our yearning for God and our free response. This offer of life restores friendship with God, makes us holy, and gives us the strength to walk in right relationship with God and with one another. Our shared Christian life, based on faith in Christ and lived out in charity, is expressed in the New Law, the law of love, grace, and freedom.

Jesus also guides us. While as Saint Paul said, "Jesus is like us in all things except sin" and thus experienced the kinds of human joys, struggles, and disappointments common to all of us, Jesus is at the same time the Divine Son of God. And it is precisely our belief in Jesus' divinity that is the foundation for all the core beliefs we hold as his disciples; he is the source of all Truth; he is the Savior of the world.

In addition to God the Father and to Jesus, the Holy Spirit guides us as well. "For what human being knows what is truly human except the human spirit that is within? So also no one comprehends what is truly God's except the Spirit of God" (1 Corinthians 2:11). It is through the Holy Spirit that we are able to know God the Father and to know Jesus, and it is through the Church that we are able to know the Holy Spirit. Jesus and the Holy Spirit work together to spread God's word. The *Catechism of the Catholic Church* says, "In their joint mission, the Son and the Holy Spirit are distinct but inseparable. To be sure, it is Christ who is seen, the visible image of the invisible God, but it is the Spirit who reveals him" (689). The Holy Spirit continues to work through all of us who are faithful people carrying on the message of Jesus.

Journal

Who are the guides in your life?
_____
_____

Why did you choose these people to be your guides?
_____
_____
_____

SYMBOL SKETCH

On a separate sheet of paper, draw your own symbol for the Trinity. You can combine symbols with which you are already familiar (the cross, fire, water) or you can create something new. You can also include symbols of other guides in your life to illustrate how all of our guides work together to help us be the best that we can be. Be prepared to explain your drawing to your classmates. At the conclusion of the presentations, display the symbols around the classroom as a reminder that our guides are always with us.

Physical laws

Many laws and rules are really descriptions of how things are and how they work. For example, "What goes up, must come down" is a simple way of describing the law of gravity, one of the most basic facts in our physical world. You obey this law all the time. Another law that you must obey is that two physical things can't occupy the same space at the same time. If you don't believe it, try walking through a closed door or a brick wall. Every time you stub a toe you are reminded of this law. You've been learning most of the physical facts or laws by trial and error from the time you were a baby. That you've survived this long is proof you've also learned to respect and obey most of them.

These rules are called *physical laws*. Physical laws are dictated by nature, describing the facts about how things are, how they work, and how they relate to each other. If we choose to disobey these physical laws, we destroy the world around us—and ourselves. Also, within all people there exists knowledge of *natural law,* the inborn sense that knows the difference between right and wrong. The great harm we've done to our world's environment is proof enough of what happens when we don't obey these laws.

Catechism Clip

The natural law, present in the heart of each man and established by reason, is universal in its precepts and its authority extends to all men. It expresses the dignity of the person and determines the basis for his fundamental rights and duties. . . . (1956)

P.L.A.Y. (PHYSICAL LAWS AND YOU)

Form a group with three other classmates. Then assign one person from your group to keep a record of the group's answers. When your teacher tells you to begin, list as many physical laws as you can think of. After three minutes, see which group has the most correct answers listed.

_____
_____
_____
_____
_____
_____
_____
_____
_____

A CONTINUING SAGA... (PART 2)

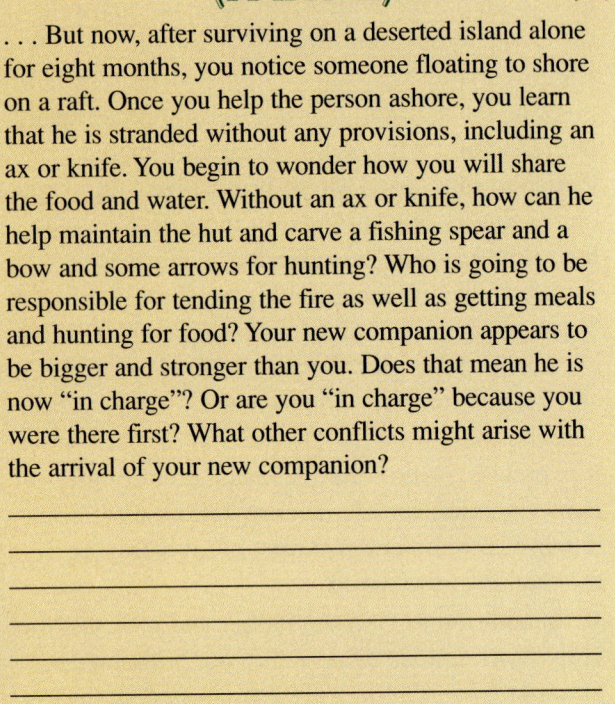

. . . But now, after surviving on a deserted island alone for eight months, you notice someone floating to shore on a raft. Once you help the person ashore, you learn that he is stranded without any provisions, including an ax or knife. You begin to wonder how you will share the food and water. Without an ax or knife, how can he help maintain the hut and carve a fishing spear and a bow and some arrows for hunting? Who is going to be responsible for tending the fire as well as getting meals and hunting for food? Your new companion appears to be bigger and stronger than you. Does that mean he is now "in charge"? Or are you "in charge" because you were there first? What other conflicts might arise with the arrival of your new companion?

_____
_____
_____
_____
_____
_____
_____
_____

Moral laws

Just as there are *physical* facts or laws that describe how physical things work and relate to each other, there are written *moral* laws that describe how people need to treat each other and relate in order to survive and to be happy together. An example of moral law would be the Ten Commandments or the ongoing teachings of our Church. Moral laws are based on the *natural moral law*—the original moral sense within all people that calls them to use **reason** to choose good and to avoid evil. While physical laws exist for our safety in the universe, the natural moral law exists for our happiness—and for the happiness of others. If you ignore the natural moral law, the result is similar to when you ignore physical laws: disorder, destruction, death.

Morality is the way we put our beliefs into action for what is good. For Christians, morality flows from our personal relationship with Christ. We strive to be good because of God's love for us and our love for God. Of their nature, some acts are always wrong because they are a choice for moral evil. Today's headlines are filled with such stories of murder, theft, and rape.

There are stories of wars and rebellions that kill innocent people. Greed and racial hatreds are causing thousands of people to starve every day. There are stories of terrorism, child abuse, drug abuse, and drive-by shootings. You can trace every one of these miseries back to the effects of original sin and moral laws that people have chosen to ignore.

The objective norms of morality are based on the natural moral law, which is expressed in the written moral laws such as the Ten Commandments, the law of love, the Beatitudes, and the ongoing teachings of the Church. Because they are an expression of the natural moral law, the Ten Commandments bring to light the essential duties and fundamental rights of all people. They teach us the true humanity of all people.

While the natural moral law is unchanging, the teaching authority of the Church interprets this law for today and assists us in the formation of a good conscience. The Church teaches that in all moral situations, we are obliged to follow our well-formed conscience. We know God's commandments through the Church and through the voice of moral conscience.

> ### IN THE NEWS...
> Find an article from the newspaper that describes a situation where someone or a group of people have chosen to ignore moral laws. Then compose a follow-up article where people following their conscience and moral laws have tried to better the situation. For example, a family's home is destroyed by fire when an arsonist sets it ablaze a week before Christmas. The family escapes unharmed but they have lost all their possessions, including their Christmas tree and presents. Reacting to the situation, a local church group begins accepting for the family monetary donations as well as clothing and toy donations.

Divine law

Before we begin our study of the Ten Commandments, let's define the word *commandment*. A commandment is a divine law, a direction from God. Surely you've seen the directions booklet you get with electronics equipment, such as a computer, a stereo, or a VCR. The directions are provided so that you can learn how to properly operate the equipment. The Ten Commandments, a prime example of divine law, function in much the same way. God provided them so that we have a set of directions to follow in order to live our lives properly. The Ten Commandments express our fundamental duties toward God and toward our neighbor—to love God and to love one another.

Just as you have the option of not reading or not following the directions that came with your new computer, you may choose not to follow the Ten Commandments. If you do not read the directions that came with your new computer, it may not work properly. For example, you might severely damage the computer if you think the mouse needs to be plugged into the motherboard inside the computer. In much the same way, if you do not read and follow the Ten Commandments, you might hurt someone, leading to the destruction of a relationship. Most importantly, you will destroy your relationship with God. Following Jesus involves following the commandments.

The Ten Commandments

The Ten Commandments (also known as the *Decalogue*, meaning "ten words") describe the basic moral law for being fully human and fully happy. They describe how things work on the spiritual level in the human community, much the way gravity describes how things work on the physical level in the physical universe.

It's just a fact that our human community depends on things such as respect for authority, respect for life, truthfulness, sharing of material goods—whether that community consists of two people or two billion people. Through the Ten Commandments, God teaches us the basic facts of what it takes to live together and be happy as human beings. Even before God revealed the Ten Commandments to Moses and the Hebrew people, the moral laws for being human and happy were operating.

In Chapter 19 of the Book of Exodus in the Bible, God appeared to Moses at the top of Mount Sinai. While Moses could not look upon the face of God, he was able to see God in the form of a thick cloud of smoke; God's voice was in the form of thunder.

Actually, God presented Moses with the Ten Commandments on two separate occasions. The first is recorded in the Book of Exodus, chapter 20, verses 1–17. After receiving the Ten Commandments the first time, Moses came down from Mount Sinai and found the Hebrew people—God's covenant people—worshiping the golden calf, a false idol. Moses was so filled with anger that he thrust the stone tablets—upon which the commandments were carved—to the ground, shattering them.

Thankfully, God is a great forgiver. He instructed Moses to cut two more stone tablets, just like the first set. Once again, Moses went to the top of Mount Sinai. God appeared in a cloud of smoke and Moses carved the words of the Decalogue onto the tablets of stone, thus renewing God's covenant with the Hebrews. (See Exodus 34:1–28.) For Moses, the Ten Commandments were carved on stone; for us, they are carved in our hearts.

Catechism Clip

Since they express man's fundamental duties towards God and towards his neighbor, the Ten Commandments reveal, in their primordial content, grave obligations. They are fundamentally immutable, and they oblige always and everywhere. No one can dispense from them. The Ten Commandments are engraved by God in the human heart. (2072)

---

1. I am the Lord, your God; you shall not have strange gods before me.
2. You shall not take the name of the Lord your God in vain.
3. Remember to keep holy the Sabbath day.
4. Honor your father and your mother.
5. You shall not kill.
6. You shall not commit adultery.
7. You shall not steal.
8. You shall not bear false witness against your neighbor.
9. You shall not covet your neighbor's wife.
10. You shall not covet your neighbor's goods.

Scripture Search

Read Exodus 19:16–20:21. Imagine that you are Moses or one of the Israelites in this scene. What feelings do you think the people are experiencing at this time?

_____
_____

Have you ever experienced these feelings at some time during your life?

_____
_____
_____

Journal

Which of the Ten Commandments seems to be the most difficult for you to follow? Why?

_____
_____
_____

What do you think could be done to change this?

_____
_____
_____

WHERE DID THIS HAPPEN?

The Bible does not provide enough information to pinpoint the exact location of Mount Sinai, also known as Mount Horeb or the "mountain of God." A 7,500-foot-high peak called *Jebel Musa*, or "mountain of Moses," located near the southern tip of the Sinai Peninsula, is considered to be the traditional location of Mount Sinai. Can you locate the Sinai Peninsula on a modern-day map?

An important agreement

We have been using the terms *covenant* and *covenant people*, but what exactly is a *covenant*? Generally speaking, a covenant is a pact, an agreement, a contract, or a set of mutual promises. After rescuing the Hebrew people from slavery in Egypt, God entered into a special relationship, or *covenant*, with them. God promised to always protect and care for the Hebrew people. For their part, the Hebrew people promised to live by the covenant, including following the Ten Commandments or instructions God revealed to them.

In a real sense, the Hebrew people needed to follow the "do"s and "don't"s of the commandments to be fully human and fully happy, even if God never formed a covenant with them. As was said before, the commandments basically describe how things are to be with our human community. But when the Hebrews entered into an agreement with God, these laws of human nature became religious laws, too, and a core part of the Hebrew religion.

The Hebrew people agreed to follow these principles as a sign and proof of their love and trust in the God who rescued them and chose them as his special people. Following the commandments was a religious duty, not just common sense.

So if they chose to ignore one of the commandments, the Hebrew people weren't just being stupid and harming the human community. They saw it as sin—that is, a rebellion against God, a rejection of God's love and friendship. If they broke these commandments, they knew they risked destroying their special friendship with God as God's chosen people.

You, too, have entered a similar religious pact or covenant with God by your Baptism. You promised to strive to follow the Ten Commandments, not out of common sense or fear, but out of love and loyalty to the God who has rescued you from death and who seeks you out as a special friend. The Ten Commandments are more than just common sense for you. Following the commandments is a religious act, a way of showing your love and respect for God. On the other hand, deliberately choosing to ignore them is sinful, a breaking of your promises to God and a rejection of God's love for you.

The first commandment God delivered to the Israelites was "I am the LORD your God, who brought you out of the land of Egypt, out of the house of slavery; you shall have no other gods before me" (Exodus 20:2–3). While the law is conditional, God's love is not. He says that he is the Lord, **but** we are to honor no other gods before him. That is a condition, or a qualification. As noted earlier, we have a choice as to whether or not we honor this covenant. The decision is ours. We know what is right. What do we do about it? The right choice is to accept the grace of God, to act as Jesus would, and to follow the guidance of the Holy Spirit.

Journal

Have you ever entered into a covenant agreement with another person? Describe the covenant.

_____
_____
_____

Scripture Search

Covenant is referred to throughout the Bible. Look up the following Scripture passages in the Bible. Explain who was involved in the covenant relationship and summarize the passage. Then answer the questions that follow.

Scripture passage	Who was involved	Summary
Genesis 9:8–17		
Exodus 19:1–9		
Exodus 34:10–28		
Jeremiah 31:31–34		

Journal

What is the difference between the old covenant and the new covenant?
_____
_____

What do these covenants say about God's willingness to forgive?
_____
_____

The Greatest Commandment

When the Pharisees heard that he had silenced the Sadducees, they gathered together, and one of them, a lawyer, asked him a question to test him. "Teacher, which commandment in the law is the greatest?" He said to him, "'You shall love the Lord your God with all your heart, and with all your soul, and with all your mind.' This is the greatest and first commandment. And a second is like it: 'You shall love your neighbor as yourself.' On these two commandments hang all the law and the prophets." (Matthew 22:34–40)

The greatest commandment that we have is to love. We are called to love God with our whole heart, soul, mind, and strength, and to love one another as much as we love ourselves. What does that mean, to love? How do we go about following this commandment? We have been given guidelines about how to love through the Ten Commandments. The Decalogue must be interpreted in light of this commandment of love. All Ten Commandments are summed up in the single sentence "You shall love your neighbor as yourself." Love does no wrong to a neighbor; therefore, love is fulfillment of the law. Jesus answered the question about the greatest

10

commandment in order to reinforce and to complement the Ten Commandments, not to eliminate or replace them. Throughout this text, we will be exploring the meaning and the mission behind the Ten Commandments.

On the flip side, the opposite of love is selfishness and lack of concern for another person's rights or happiness. This inclination to sin is one of the effects of original sin. In real life, this selfishness can take the forms of lying, stealing, prejudice, violence, greed, and indifference. These acts can lead us away from our covenant relationship with God. They are the kinds of things the commandments instruct us to avoid. Perhaps that's the best way of all to view the commandments—as detailed instructions about how to love God, others, and yourself.

A CONTINUING SAGA... (PART 3)

Write a conclusion to the story of being stranded on a deserted island with your new companion. The climax of the story should build upon the conflicts that you described earlier that might arise. How will you resolve these conflicts by following the commandment to love your neighbor as yourself?

Scripture Search

Jesus traveled all over Galilee, teaching and preaching the good news of God and the kingdom of heaven. One day, Jesus went up on a hillside, where his disciples gathered around him. He spoke these words about finding true blessedness, which are now known as the Beatitudes. Take a few minutes to read Matthew 5:1–12. After reading the passage, rewrite each beatitude in your own words.

What do the Beatitudes tell us about true blessedness? They reiterate the greatest commandment of all: We are called to love God and to love one another. In loving God and in loving each other, we find true blessedness. The Ten Commandments and the Beatitudes supply directions for how to love and to serve one another.

More directions!

Feeling overwhelmed? Don't be. It's not as difficult as it looks. You already have a good idea of what is right and what is wrong. Yet knowing what is right and doing what is right are two separate and distinct ideas. Let's take a look at your own similarities and differences between knowing and doing.

What is the right thing to do?	Situation	What would I actually do?
	1. You are staying at a friend's house from early Saturday afternoon until Sunday evening. Your friend is not Catholic. What should you do about attending Mass?	
	2. It's Friday evening. Your friends pick you up at your house to go to a movie. At the theater, your friends decide to go to a later movie than planned. You know that by going to this later movie, you will not make curfew.	
	3. You and your friends are at the music store at the mall. When the clerk isn't looking, your friends stuff some compact discs in a bag. They walk over to you and begin pressuring you to steal a CD you've been wanting for a long time.	

The first situation relates to the third commandment: "Remember to keep holy the Lord's day." One of the laws of the Church, as a covenant people, is to go to Mass every Saturday evening or Sunday and on holy days of obligation. We know that is the right thing to do.

The second situation applies to the fourth commandment: "Honor your father and your mother." Part of the natural moral law is that good is to be done. We know that it is right to obey our parents.

The third situation corresponds to the seventh commandment: "You shall not steal." Another part of natural moral law is that evil is to be avoided. By not taking what does not belong to us, we are avoiding evil; we are doing what is right.

As you can see, you already have some understanding of the Ten Commandments. You know that it is wrong to skip Mass, to disappoint your parents, and to steal. However, we have also discussed that *knowing* what is right and *doing* what is right are two different things. The chapters ahead are designed to help you bridge the gap between knowing and doing.

Scripture Search

Read the following Scripture passages and be prepared to discuss how each relates to natural moral law (inborn sense of right and wrong) and to moral laws (written laws). Jot down your thoughts in the space provided.

• Romans 10:4

• Philippians 2:12–13

Pause to Pray

God our Father,
Thank you for the fullness of life you show us through your love. Continue to guide us and protect us in everything we do. Help us understand that your laws are given to us because you want us to be happy and have eternal life. Amen.

Journal

Describe a time when God guided and protected you.
_____
_____
_____

Describe one thing you will do this week to show your love for others.
_____
_____
_____

Homework

Read Exodus 20:1–17, the passage where God presents Moses with the Ten Commandments. On a separate sheet of paper, summarize in your own words each commandment. Then write a brief story for each commandment in which that commandment is broken. This assignment will help prepare you for the chapters ahead. Be sure to bring your assignment with you to class each time so that you can refer to it when studying each commandment.

Chapter 2
I Am the Lord Your God

CORNERSTONE OF LIFE

The first commandment is the foundation for the other commandments. Draw a diagram of this foundation and the remainder of the commandments that are built upon it.

Now draw a diagram of the foundation upon which your values and morals are built. Who and what helped you form your belief system?

The beginning

"I am the LORD your God, who brought you out of the land of Egypt, out of the house of slavery; you shall have no other gods before me" (Exodus 20:2–3). This phrase, though very simple, is extremely important. It signifies the beginning of the Decalogue, or the Ten Commandments. It is the cornerstone, or foundation, for all the other commandments. This commandment seeks to help you form a solid, loving relationship with God. If you place the cornerstone properly, the rest of the building goes up level and straight. If you form the right kind of relationship with God, all the other commandments fall into place.

The reverse is also true, of course. If a cornerstone is crooked, the whole building goes up crooked. And if your relationship with God is weak or off-center, you will tend to misunderstand or ignore the other commandments, too. So in this chapter we need to explore just what the first commandment really means and what it is asking you to do.

Side Note

When Moses went to the top of Mount Sinai, he received the Ten Commandments carved on two stone tablets along with other laws and a plan for a worship site. Since the Israelites were going to be traveling to their new home in Canaan, they needed a way to transport the stone tablets. God instructed them to build a box made from acacia wood, covered with gold inside and out, and measuring 90" X 90" X 54". The box, which became known as the ark of the covenant, was kept at the center of the Israelites' camp as they wandered in the wilderness. Inside the ark, the Israelites kept the stone tablets on which the Ten Commandments were written, a pot of manna (which had fed the Israelites while they were wandering in the desert), and Aaron's rod. All of these were reminders of God's love for his chosen people.

Where is the ark of the covenant today? It disappeared when Nebuchadnezzar's armies invaded Jerusalem in 586 B.C.E.

Scripture Search

Read Exodus 27:1–8. Using the description of the ark of the covenant in this Scripture passage, draw a representation of what you believe the ark looked like. When everyone is finished, compare everyone's drawings and comment on similarities and differences.

It's about faith, hope, and charity

The words *I am the Lord your God* say it all. The God of the Hebrews is the one and only God. This means that everything and everyone depend upon God for existence and for happiness. Nothing or no one is more important than God. Accepting this fact is the heart of the first commandment.

This commandment calls you to believe in the one and only true God and to believe in God's love for you. This is *faith*. Our moral life has its source of faith in God who reveals his love to us.

The first commandment also calls you to trust in God above all else and in God's promise always to love, care for, and, when necessary, forgive you. This is *hope*. We must hope that we are given the capacity to love God in return and to act in conformity with the commandments of charity.

Scripture Search

Read Luke 15:11–32. One of the sins against hope is *presumption*. There are two types of presumption. The first type is when a person hopes he or she can save himself or herself without help from God. The second type of presumption is when a person hopes he or she can obtain forgiveness without conversion, and glory without merit. Would you say that the prodigal son, the one who left his home, squandered all of his money, and then returned home to a hero's welcome, demonstrated presumption? If so, which type of presumption? If not, why? Cite passages from the Gospel of Luke to support your answer.

_____
_____
_____
_____
_____
_____
_____
_____

Journal

Where have you seen examples of presumption?
_____
_____

Have you ever taken full credit for successes that should have been attributed (in some way) to God?
_____
_____

Have you ever thought about doing something wrong, thinking that you could simply ask for forgiveness later?
_____
_____

Finally, this commandment includes the call and the obligation to respond with love to divine *charity*. It directs us to love God above all things for God's own sake and to love our neighbors as ourselves for the love of God. Charity is the virtue that calls us to be kind to those who need our help. It is an intrinsic part of the first commandment.

In order to truly honor the Lord our God, we must also honor all people. We have many opportunities to exhibit charity on a daily basis. It is our conscious choice to take advantage of such opportunities. It is important for us to do kind acts for one another. Jesus said, "Whatever you do to the least of my people, that you do unto me." When we honor one another, we in turn honor God.

So this commandment calls you to believe in God, to hope in God, and to love God above all else. On the surface, this commandment is easy enough to understand. And it may also seem easy enough to follow. It's one thing to believe in, to trust, and to love God. It's an entirely different matter to believe in, to trust, and to love God *above all else*. It's the *above all else* that is the real challenge of this commandment.

Journal

How have you shown charity toward someone in the last week?
_____
_____
_____

#1 PRIORITY

Make a list of five idols in your life. Then list how you can change your lifestyle to lessen the importance of these idols in your life. How can you strengthen the importance of God and your faith in your life?

Scripture Search

Not even the Israelites were exempt from worshiping false gods. In fact, as mentioned in chapter 1, while Moses was up on Mount Sinai receiving God's commandments, the Israelites were at the foot of the mountain, dancing around a golden calf. Take a moment to read Exodus 32:1–5.

• Why did the Israelites ask Aaron to make them a god?

• Why did Aaron build the golden calf?

• What should Aaron have done?

• Why didn't he?

THE BEATITUDES

Happy are those who trust in God.

Happy are those who comfort the lonely and the sad.

Happy are those who are gentle and kind.

Happy are those who pray often.

Happy are those who treat others fairly.

Happy are those who forgive and forget.

Happy are those who love God.

Happy are those who are joyful.

Happy are those who live in peace.

—*Adapted from Matthew 5:3–12*

Try to name six TV shows, movies, or popular songs that promote the kinds of values contained in the Beatitudes. After each show, movie, or song, write the value it promotes. Compare your list with those of the others in your group.

TV show, movie, or popular song **Beatitude value**

Superstition and magic

One way you can give things and other people more importance than they deserve is to treat them as if they had some God-like power.

That's what superstition and magic are about—thinking certain objects, words, actions, or people have special powers to make your wishes come true.

I WISH I MAY, I WISH I MIGHT . . .

Imagine that you have unearthed an ancient golden lamp in your own backyard. When you open the lamp, a genie is released. The genie promises to grant you three wishes in gratitude for releasing him from the lamp. What three wishes would you ask of the genie?

1.

2.

3.

Often superstitions are harmless enough. Have you ever had a lucky penny or a lucky rabbit's foot? If so, what made you think that it was "lucky"? Perhaps it seemed that good things happened to you when you carried your lucky penny or rabbit's foot.

When we begin to put false hope in such charms, it violates the first commandment. *Things* do not bring good luck; faith in God supplies true courage and strength.

But if you ever really *believed* that the penny or rabbit's foot had some mysterious power, you were moving toward a kind of idolatry. You are giving God-like powers to an object or an action. Suppose you have an important math test coming up. Instead of reading the assigned material, you walk into class on test day wearing your lucky hat. Will your lucky hat help your performance on the test? Of course not! If you read the material in advance, however, and pray that God will be with you as you take the test, you will have a much better chance of doing well on the exam.

Belief in palm readers, fortune-tellers, ouija boards, horoscopes, and tarot cards are also forms of idolatry. If you really believe such people or things have the power to foresee the future (a power only God has) and live your life according to their predictions, you are involved in a kind of idolatry.

Becoming involved in magic is a sin against the first commandment as well. This does not refer to the sleight-of-hand magic magicians use to saw people in half or to pull a rabbit out of a hat. Rather, the practices of magic by which one attempts to gain and to use supernatural powers over others is a violation of the first commandment. These practices are even more condemned when the intention of these powers is to harm others.

Journal

Why do you think many people are drawn to palm readers, fortune-tellers, ouija boards, and tarot cards?
_____
_____
_____

How would you explain to these people that such practices violate the first commandment?
_____
_____
_____

Prayer can help

Prayer helps us perform acts of faith, hope, and charity. Prayer keeps our hearts focused on the Ten Commandments. There are five types of prayer:

1. Prayers of blessing
2. Prayers of petition, asking God for forgiveness
3. Prayers of intercession, asking God for something on the behalf of others
4. Prayers of thanksgiving
5. Prayers of praise

We utilize different prayers for different purposes. You can pray anytime, anywhere. You can pray using formal prayers, such as the Lord's Prayer or the Hail Mary, and you can pray using informal prayers, such as talking to God as you walk to school or get ready for bed. No matter what the form, pray. Prayer gives us the strength and the courage to follow God's commands.

DEAR GOD, I WISH I MAY, I WISH I MIGHT . . .

Do you remember what three wishes you chose to make if a genie were to grant them? Write your wishes below.

1.

2.

3.

Now think back to the discussion of the idols many people worship today. Do any of your wishes reflect one of these idols, something that people treat as if it were more important than God, such as money, a car, or a successful career? If your wishes reflect one of these idols, make another wish and write it below.

For each wish, write a short prayer of petition asking God for strength and guidance in helping to achieve your wish.

PRAYER PLANNING

Select a partner. With your partner, select one of the five types of prayer and write a prayer. After you have finished writing your prayers, you and your classmates can sign up on a schedule for a class time in which you can lead the class in your prayer on that day.

Sacred images

While it is against the first commandment to worship false gods and to honor lucky charms, it is not against the first commandment to *venerate*, or to show respect for, sacred images such as crosses, religious medallions, and rosaries. Some of the most common images of this sort are medallions, or symbols, of the saints. Many Catholics have a Saint Jude medallion or a statue of Saint Francis of Assisi. It is perfectly okay to honor the saints, or to honor the crucifix. Showing respect for sacred images is a part of our faith tradition. These items should lead us to imitating virtues of the saints and witnessing to our faith.

Sometimes, however, people believe that a medallion or a rosary brings good luck, that as long as they have that particular charm, nothing will happen to them. This is when honoring the saints turns into idol worship. Remember, strength and courage come from God, not from things.

MIRACULOUS MEDALS

If you have a medallion or a statue of a saint at home, ask permission to bring it in and share it with the class. Describe which saint it is, what he or she did, and why it is important to you.

Scripture Search

As a class, divide yourselves into three groups. Each group should be assigned one of the following three Scripture passages. As a group, first read the assigned passage. Talk about and record what it means; then discuss ways in which the passage applies to your lives. As a group, compose a skit showing an example of how the passage is present in your everyday lives.

Scripture passage	What it means	How it applies to my life
Matthew 6:19–21		
Matthew 6:22–23		
Matthew 6:24–39		

Pause to Pray

Dear Lord,
You are the Lord our God, who has brought us out of the slavery of sin. Help us cast aside false gods and set our sights on you alone. Guide us as we strive to express faith, hope, and charity to those around us. We ask this in Jesus' name.
Amen.

Journal

Think about the way that you live your life. What does the way that you spend your time, your effort, and your money say about you? Are your priorities consistent with how the first commandment calls us to live? If so, how? If not, what could you do differently?

___
___
___
___

Homework

1. Look back at your homework from chapter 1. You were to read each of the Ten Commandments, then put each commandment into your own words. How did you phrase the first commandment? Now that you have completed chapter 2, is there anything that you would like to add? Take this time to record any changes here in your textbook.

2. Create a poster below that states the first commandment. Then using words, pictures, and symbols, decorate the poster with reasons why God is to be number one in our lives.

Chapter 3
You Shall Not Take the Name of the Lord Your God In Vain
Remember To Keep Holy the Sabbath Day

RESPECT

When it comes to dealing with other people and special events, how would you define *respect*? Using the acronym below, write a word or phrase after each letter that describes what you believe respect is all about.

R _____

E _____

S _____

P _____

E _____

C _____

T _____

CALLED BY NAME

God calls each one of us by name. Everyone's name is sacred. It demands respect as a sign of the dignity of the one who bears it. An extension of the second commandment, which calls us to honor God's name, is the call to honor all people. Knowing everyone is called by name by God, we need to extend the same respect toward others.

Do you know how you received your name? Perhaps you were named after a relative or a saint. If you do not know, go home tonight and ask how your parent(s) decided upon the name that you have. Then answer the following questions. Be ready to share your answers in class.

How did you get your name?
_____
_____

What does your name mean?
_____
_____

What does your name say about you?
_____
_____

Do you think that your name suits you? Why or why not?
_____
_____

Promises, promises

An *oath* is a solemn vow to God that you will speak the truth or keep a promise, and it is not to be taken lightly. A promise is not to be used in order to put God to the test. For example, it is wrong to say, "Lord, if you let me do well on this test, I promise that I will always study hard in the future." That is called *bargaining*, and it has no place in true faith in God.

Sometimes our siblings ask us to make false oaths. If a brother or a sister breaks a lamp while playing ball in the house, even though he or she knows that it is wrong, he or she might ask you to "swear to God" that you will not tell your mom or your dad. This is an example of a false oath; it is calling upon the name of the Lord to protect a deceitful act.

Other times, our friends might ask us to make a false oath. If a friend confides in you that he or she has an eating disorder, he or she might ask you to "swear to God" that you will not tell anyone. While you may think that such an oath is honoring your friendship with this person, it is actually putting your friend in danger. If you honor such a false oath by withholding information that could be harmful to another person, you are committing a sin. If you do not help your friend seek help, you could be dealing with something far worse than a false oath!

Oaths and perjury

"Do you swear to tell the truth, the whole truth, and nothing but the truth, so help you God?" This is one of the most famous oaths in our society. It is spoken when a person approaches the witness stand during a trial, and it signifies that what the person is about to say is the absolute truth, to the best of his or her knowledge. Saint Augustine said, "[God's] name is great when spoken with respect for the greatness of his majesty. God's name is holy when said with veneration and fear of offending him." Because a person's testimony in a court of law is given in honor of God and out of respect for the truth, the last part of this oath is acceptable. *Perjury* occurs when someone willingly provides false testimony when he or she is under oath.

Side Note

In Old Testament times, it was common for Jewish people to swear oaths by touching a sacred object or by putting a hand on the Torah. By Jesus' time, oath taking was being abused, so he discouraged people from swearing by heaven or earth. Matthew 5:37 states, "Let your word be 'Yes, Yes' or 'No, No'; anything more than this comes from the evil one."

UNDER OATH

Form a small group of four people. In your group, design two skits. In one skit, show how an oath can be used correctly. In another skit, show an example of how to handle a false oath.

Scripture Search

Satan even tried to put Jesus to the test. Read Luke 4:1–13; then answer the following questions.

• What does Satan want Jesus to do?

• Why?

• How does Jesus respond?

Jesus knew that promising to honor Satan was a false oath for him. Jesus had the faith and the courage to turn away and honor his oath to love God with all of his heart, with all of his soul, and with all of his mind. He honored the great commandment.

Sign of the Cross

When we pray, we, too, honor the great commandment. We also honor the second commandment by using the name of the Lord when we pray. When we pray the Sign of the Cross, we say, "In the name of the Father, and of the Son, and of the Holy Spirit." This, too, shows honor and respect for the name of the Lord.

At Mass each week, during the introductory rites, we begin the celebration by making the sign of the cross. The priest then welcomes the congregation in the name of the Lord. He says, "The grace of our Lord Jesus Christ and the love of God and the fellowship of the Holy Spirit be with you all," to which we respond, "And also with you." This greeting shows respect for God and honors the Trinity as the central part of the celebration of the Mass.

Likewise, at the end of each Mass, during the concluding rite, the priest prays, "May almighty God bless you, the Father, and the Son, and the Holy Spirit," to which we respond, "Amen" (meaning "I believe"). During this blessing, we once again mark ourselves with the sign of the cross, expressing honor and reverence for the name of the Lord. Remember this the next time you make the sign of the cross.

The Sign of the Cross strengthens us in temptations and difficulties. If you are tempted to use God's name in vain, pray the Sign of the Cross as a reminder of your faith. If you are struggling with a false oath, pray the Sign of the Cross as a reminder of the real truth.

Journal
In addition to the sign of the cross, when is another time during liturgy when the faithful "mark" themselves? What does it mean?
_____
_____
_____
_____
_____

A reminder of God's creation

The third commandment directs us to honor God by honoring the Sabbath. For most Christians, we honor the Sabbath on Sunday. Those of the Jewish faith, however, honor the Sabbath on Saturday. The purpose of the Sabbath remains the same: it commemorates God's creation of the world. "For in six days the LORD made heaven and earth, the sea, and all that is in them, but rested the seventh day; therefore the LORD blessed the sabbath day and consecrated it" (Exodus 20:11).

Every Sunday, we celebrate the the Israelites' release from bondage in Egypt. Deuteronomy 5:15 reads, "Remember that you were a slave in the land of Egypt, and the LORD your God brought you out from there with a mighty hand and an outstretched arm; therefore the LORD your God commanded you to keep the sabbath day." Every time that we celebrate the Mass, we are recreating the Passover supper, when Moses and the Israelites were spared destruction because of God's favor. Thus the Sabbath is for the Lord, holy and set apart for the praise of God, God's work of creation, and God's saving actions on behalf of Israel.

The book of Exodus outlines the events leading to the Passover. The original Passover event is described in Exodus 12:1–14. At the Last Supper, Jesus and his disciples were honoring the Passover feast. Celebrating the Israelites' release from bondage is a central idea of the Mass and of the Sabbath as a whole.

The Sabbath separated the Israelites from work and all other ordinary activity (Exodus 35:2–3); thus it reminded them of Israel's separation from the nations around them and of their relation to God as a covenant people. When we honor the Sabbath, we also honor the Lord. We remember, we celebrate, and we believe that God established a covenant with the Israelites.

Every Sunday we celebrate the Paschal mystery, Jesus' saving death and resurrection. Jesus is the new Paschal Lamb as we celebrate the Eucharistic meal and sacrifice that Jesus gave us at the Last Supper, his last Passover meal.

Scripture Search

"This is the day that the LORD has made; let us rejoice and be glad in it." (Psalm 118:24)

List five ways in which you can set apart Sunday from the rest of the week:

1.
2.
3.
4.
5.

If God "rested and was refreshed" on the seventh day, we, too, ought to "rest" and should let others, especially those who are poor, "be refreshed." The Sabbath brings everyday work to a halt and provides a respite. It is a day of protest against the servitude of work and the worship of money. Although you could cite several times when Jesus was accused of violating the Sabbath law, remember that Christ never failed to respect the holiness of this day. With compassion, Jesus declared the Sabbath for doing good rather than harm, for saving life rather than killing.

Scripture Search

Read the following stories of people accusing Jesus of violating the Sabbath laws: Luke 13:10–17 and Mark 3:1–6.

Who did Jesus heal?
_____
_____

How did others react?
_____
_____

What was Jesus' response?
_____
_____

What would your reaction have been?
_____
_____

The Sunday Eucharist

The Sunday celebration of the Lord's day and the Eucharist is at the heart of the Catholic Church. Saint Paul's Letter to the Hebrews reminds the faithful "not neglecting to meet together, as is the habit of some, but encouraging one another" (10:25). As Catholics, our faithful meet in *parishes*, definite communities within a particular Church under the pastoral care of a priest. It is the place where all the faithful can gather together for the Sunday celebration of the Eucharist. We celebrate with our risen Lord. Every Sunday, in a way, is a little Easter. This cannot happen alone at one's home, for missing would be the union of minds, the accord of souls, the bond of charity, and the prayers of the priests.

The precept (law) of the Church specifies this more precisely: "You shall attend Mass on Sundays and on holy days of obligation and rest from servile labor." The Sunday Eucharist is the foundation and confirmation of all Christian practice. For this reason the faithful are obliged to participate in the Eucharist on days of obligation, unless excused for a serious reason. Those who deliberately fail in this obligation commit a grave sin.

LEARNING ABOUT YOUR PARISH

Using parish resources or by interviewing staff members in your parish, research the following information:

Name of parish:
_____

Year founded:
_____

Mission statement:
_____
_____
_____

Current number of families:
_____

Current pastor(s) and staff:
_____
_____
_____
_____

Other:
_____
_____
_____

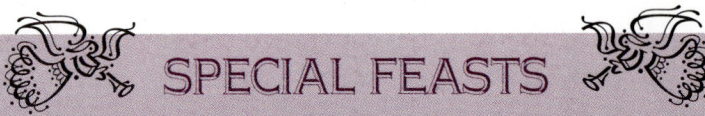

SPECIAL FEASTS

Holy days of obligation are special feasts on which Catholics who have reached the age of reason are seriously obliged, as on Sundays, to assist at Mass and to avoid unnecessary work. Can you match the holy days of obligation with their dates of worship?

___ 1. January 1   A. All Saints' Day

___ 2. Forty days after Easter   B. Christmas

___ 3. August 15   C. Mary's Immaculate Conception

___ 4. November 1   D. Mary, Mother of God

___ 5. December 8   E. Mary's Assumption

___ 6. December 25   F. Ascension Thursday

Can you explain what each holy day of obligation celebrates?

All Saints' Day:
_____
_____
Christmas:
_____
_____
Mary's Immaculate Conception:
_____
_____
Mary, Mother of God:
_____
_____
Mary's Assumption:
_____
_____
Ascension Thursday:
_____
_____

Participation in the communal celebration of the Sunday Eucharist is a testimony of belonging and of being faithful to Christ and to his Church. The faithful give witness by this to their communion in faith and charity. Together they testify to God's holiness and their hope of salvation. They strengthen one another under the guidance of the Holy Spirit.

On Sundays and other holy days of obligation, the faithful are to refrain from engaging in work or activities that hinder the worship owed to God. Sunday is traditionally consecrated by Christian piety to good works and humble service of the sick, the infirm, and the elderly. Christians also sanctify Sunday by devoting time and care to their families and relatives, which is often difficult to do on other days of the week.

Journal
How does your family celebrate Sundays as a day "set apart" from the rest of the week? *or* How would you like your family to celebrate Sundays as a day "set apart" from the rest of the week?

_____
_____
_____
_____
_____
_____
_____
_____

Setting priorities straight

Do you know any people who only talk to you when they need something? Do you help them? Why or why not? How do you react when you see them or hear them? Such people have a tendency to aggravate us; yet think of your own relationship with God. Do you talk with him on a regular basis, or do you only pray in times of trouble, when you are in need of something?

Similarly, it is interesting to note how many people come late to and/or leave Mass early. If God is truly a priority in our lives, we should make the effort to make time for our faith. Like any relationship, our relationship with God takes time and effort. If we do not devote at least one hour to God each week, we are making a statement about the role of faith in our lives. When we are invited to the house of a friend, we make the effort to be on time and to be a courteous guest. The same holds true for going to the house of the Lord. When you go the house of a friend, you take part in conversation; you interact with other people. When you go to church, you should also strive to take part and to be an active "guest" by responding to the prayers and by singing. You give thanks to a friend who has been a hospitable host; remember to say thanks to God, too!

Side Note
During the time of the Israelites, society upheld very strict penalties for blasphemy and for not keeping holy the Sabbath. Since both of these were considered to be crimes against God and against human life, they carried with them a death sentence. This sentence was usually carried out by stoning the offender to death.

SUCCESSFUL RELATIONSHIPS

What makes a successful relationship? List below the qualities of a successful relationship. After looking over your list, write a description of a successful relationship in your life. Who does it involve? What makes it work? Then think about your relationship with God. What qualities on your list apply to your relationship with God? Which do not? Describe some ways in which you can improve your relationship with God.

_____
_____
_____
_____

Scripture Search

Each of these Scripture passages relates to the second or third commandment. Read each passage and be prepared to explain how each relates to its respective commandment.

                        Second Commandment   **Third Commandment**

Isaiah 43:1–7

Matthew 5:33–37

Romans 4:13–25

Deuteronomy 5:12–15

Matthew 6:5–15

Matthew 7:7–12

Pause to Pray

Dear Lord,
We are not afraid, for we know that you are with us. You have called us each by name. Help us honor you in all that we say and in all that we do. We ask this through Christ our Lord.
Amen.

Journal

Does it bother you to show reverence and respect in public toward God? If so, why do you think that is?

Does going to Mass, or "keeping holy the Sabbath," affect the rest of your week? If so, in what way(s)? If not, why not?

Whom do you worship?

The first commandment directs us to worship God and God alone. If a person believes in and worships more than one god, he or she is called a *polytheist*. Polytheism is the belief and worship of more than one god. This practice has been present throughout history. The most famous examples of polytheism come to us from Greek, Roman, and Norse mythology. The ancient Greeks, Romans, and Norse believed in an entire community of gods and goddesses to whom they prayed for favors and blessings. Stories or myths about these gods and goddesses were created to explain basic truths and events in life. For example, the Norse, from ancient Scandinavia, believed that the god Thor made thunder and lightning by throwing a hammer at his enemies. But the ancient Greeks believed that the lightning bolt was a weapon used by the god Zeus. As Christians, we know and understand that God is the basic truth. We do not need to explain why thunder and lightning occur because we know that is a part of God's design for the world.

The first commandment directs us to avoid false gods and idol worship. What do you picture when you hear the word *idol*? Do you picture a statue? Perhaps a medallion? False gods and idols can take many forms. You may think that because you do not bow down to such a statue or medallion that you do not worship other gods. Let's think about this carefully.

The first commandment says you shouldn't treat anything as if it were more important than God. When you do treat someone or something as if that person or that item were more important than God, you actually have established a false god. That's idolatry. It's one thing to know God is the most important; it's another thing to act that way.

What are the other "gods" in your life? What "idols" do you serve? Today's idols (things people treat as if they were more important than God) are most likely to be things such as a successful career, a lot of money, a great body, popularity, the "right" clothes, a big car, and power or fame. And video games, sports, and music can all become idols if you place their importance above everything else in your life. "No one can serve two masters; for a slave will either hate the one and love the other, or be devoted to the one and despise the other. You cannot serve God and wealth" (Matthew 6:24).

Believe it or not, many people do "worship" things like money, popularity, good looks, and power. They know there is only one God; they really believe it. But in their daily lives they look to and trust in things and people more than God to give them their happiness. Their main focus is not on God.

Think about your daily schedule. When you wake up, what is your morning routine? Are you more likely to turn on the stereo or to say a morning prayer? On Sunday, do you look forward to going to Mass, or are you more concerned with playing basketball? These are just a few examples of how other "gods" can play an important role in your life, perhaps displacing God and your faith. The first commandment is really about keeping your priorities straight. Success, wealth, health, and fame are all good things, important things. But they are just things. They are not as good or important as the God who creates them and keeps them in existence. Whenever you treat something in your life as if it were better or more important than God, you are getting your priorities messed up.

RANDOM ACTS OF KINDNESS

There is a campaign in our world for people to practice random acts of kindness. Random means the acts are done without seeking a reward or recognition. Perhaps you've seen or read the books telling of people's kindness to others. The following is one excerpt from *Random Acts of Kindness* (Conari Press, 1993):

When I was going through a very difficult time, someone called me up and played piano music for me on my answering machine. It made me feel very loved—and I never discovered who had done it.

In small groups, come up with ten random acts that could be performed at home and ten at school. Share your ideas with the whole class. In the coming weeks, notice when you see others performing random acts of kindness and work to perform some of your own!

Scripture Search

Many stories of faith, hope, and charity are recorded in the Bible. Read the following passages, summarize each passage, identify to which virtue the passage relates (faith, hope, or charity), and describe how each story relates to the first commandment.

Scripture passage	Summary	Virtue	How does this story relate to the first commandment?
Hebrews 11:1–3, 23–29			
Matthew 6:1–4			
2 Timothy 2:3–13			

17

It's all about respect

The second and third commandments—*"You shall not take the name of the Lord your God in vain"* (Exodus 20:7) and *"Remember to keep holy the Sabbath day"* (Exodus 20:8–11)—center on respect for God. As Christians, we need to reverence God's name and to set aside the Lord's day. Building upon the first commandment of loving only one God, these commandments instruct people on *how* to show such love: honoring the name of God and keeping holy the Sabbath.

HOLY IS GOD'S NAME

The second commandment directs us to show respect for God by prescribing respect for the Lord's name. The name of God has been confided only to those who believe, and for this reason, no one must abuse it. Believers are not to use the Lord's name in their speech except to bless, praise, and glorify it. By holding God's name sacred in our speech, we are respecting not only the name but the whole mystery of God revealed.

The second commandment not only forbids the abuse of God's name (including every improper use of the names of God and Jesus), but also of the Virgin Mary and all the saints.

Journal

We all like to have people show respect for us and for our names. If you have siblings, how does it feel when someone calls you by one of their names instead of your own? Have you ever been given a nickname that you didn't care to have? How did you react?

Blasphemy

Blasphemy is directly opposed to the second commandment. *Blasphemy* occurs when someone shows irreverence, or disrespect, for God or for sacred images. Such disrespect, whether expressed in an inward or outward fashion, is serious. Swearing—using the name of the Lord in vain—is blasphemy. It is not "cool"; it is sinful. Blasphemy is contrary to the respect due God and God's holy name.

People should not tolerate such irreverence. Even college and professional sports teams acknowledge the importance of avoiding the use of foul language. What happens when an athlete uses disrespectful language toward a referee during a game? He or she is ejected from the game and often receives a rather hefty fine. Why should God expect any less?

Journal

Do you ever swear? _____
If so, when is the last time that you used the name of the Lord in vain? _____
_____

Why did you do it? _____
_____

Who was with you? _____
_____

Is swearing something that you do only in certain contexts, with certain people? _____
_____

Take a look at your patterns of behavior; then list some more appropriate ways to express your anger or your disappointment. _____
_____
_____

Side Note

When the Jewish people made the decision to record their experiences in the Scriptures, communities of scribes were formed. It was the duty of each scribe to record the text perfectly. Scribes took their job very seriously, being extremely careful not to commit blasphemy against God.

Before he began his work each day, the scribe would test his reed pen by dipping it in ink and writing the name *Amalek*, then crossing it out (cf. Deuteronomy 25:19). Then he would say, "I am writing the Torah in the name of its sanctity." The scribe would read a sentence in the manuscript he was copying, repeat it aloud, and then write it. Each time he came to the name of God, he would say, "I am writing the name of God for the holiness of His name." If he made an error in writing God's name, he had to destroy the entire sheet of papyrus or vellum that he was using. (Packer and White, *Nelson's Illustrated Encyclopedia of Bible Facts*)

What's in a name?

In the Old Testament, names were very important to the Hebrew people. A name told a great deal about the person that it represented. Jewish people believed that they must first know a person's name before they could know the person. As time progressed, a child's name was selected to honor a servant of God, similar to how we now name a child after a saint. For example, the name *Jesus* is a Greek form of the Hebrew name *Joshua*, which means "salvation of Yahweh."

Notice how a child's name can be selected to honor another person. The name of the Lord is the embodiment of everything that is good, pure, and honorable. To use the Lord's name to show anger or hatred toward another person or situation is completely inappropriate and disrespectful.

Homework

1. Look back at your homework from chapter 1. You were to read each of the Ten Commandments, and then put each commandment into your own words. How did you phrase the second and third commandments? Now that you have completed chapter 3, is there anything that you would like to add? Take this time to record any changes in the space below.

2. We have discussed how the second and third commandments, like the first, are examples of divine law: they deal directly with God. Over the years, people have changed in how they observe these two commandments in particular. Arrange to meet with a grandparent or with an elderly person from your parish (perhaps someone who is in a nursing home). Share with this person what you have learned about these commandments. Ask the person about his or her own understanding. Find out how people honor these commandments differently today than they did in the past. For example, fifty years ago, stores were never open on Sundays. How would this affect your life today? Record below what you learn. Share your findings with your classmates.

Chapter 4
Honor Your Father and Mother

WHAT MAKES PARENTS OR GUARDIANS UNIQUE?

Think about your parents or guardians for a moment. What is it that makes them special, unique? If you could design a mother and a father, what qualities would they possess? Below, list the qualities of a good parent or guardian.

The fourth commandment is unique

The fourth commandment, "Honor your father and your mother, so that your days may be long in the land that the LORD your God is giving you" (Exodus 20:12), is special for many reasons. First of all, it opens the second tablet of the Decalogue. In addition, it is the only commandment that carries with it a promise. God promises that if you honor your father and your mother, then you will live a long and prosperous life in the Lord. God has willed that, after belief in one God, we should honor our parents or guardians to whom we owe life and who have handed on to us the knowledge of our faith. In addition, we are obliged to honor and respect all those whom God, for our good, has vested with such authority.

AUTHORITY FIGURES

Name persons in our society who have authority.
_____
_____
_____
_____

How do people show respect for these authority figures?
_____
_____
_____
_____

At times, how do people show disrespect for these authority figures?
_____
_____
_____
_____

God is our father

One day, one of Jesus' disciples said, "Lord, teach us to pray." Jesus replied with the words of the Lord's Prayer (Luke 11:1–4):

He was praying in a certain place, and after he had finished, one of his disciples said to him, "Lord, teach us to pray, as John taught his disciples." He said to them, "When you pray, say: Father, hallowed be your name. Your kingdom come. Give us each day our daily bread. And forgive us our sins, for we ourselves forgive everyone indebted to us. And do not bring us to the time of trial."

In this prayer, we address God as "our Father." We have already discussed how we are called to honor and to respect God. Our parents and guardians are part of the embodiment of God on earth. And so, we are called to honor and to respect our mother and our father.

The Christian family

The purpose of a Christian marriage is procreation. When a couple meets with a priest to arrange a wedding ceremony, the priest asks them if they are open and willing to accepting children. After a couple is married, it is considered to be a great honor to be blessed with children.

Once a couple has been blessed with children, they have established a family. Because a family is a community of faith, hope, and love, it is called a *domestic church*. The Christian family is a communion of persons, a sign and image of the communion of the Father and the Son in the Holy Spirit. The family is called to partake in daily prayer, acts of charity, and works of evangelization (spreading the gospel message).

CHURCH

Think for a moment about the concept of Church. What are the qualities of a Church community? Write them below. Now think about the concept of family. What qualities of a Church are found in a family? Record those below as well.

Elements of a Church   **How these elements are part of a family**

What kinds of elements did you find overlapping? Does that surprise you?

It is important to cherish your family. From this domestic church, you learn your values and your morals. You learn to worship God. You learn to make good use of your freedom.

Journal

What are some of the values and morals you have learned from your parents or guardians?
_____
_____
_____
_____
_____

What values and morals will you want to pass on to your children?
_____
_____
_____
_____
_____
_____

THE HOUSE THAT LOVE BUILDS

Both a physical church and a domestic church are built with love and support. To take a closer look at this framework, form groups of four. In each group, use one deck of cards to build a house of cards. Be prepared to answer the following questions:

• Was it difficult to build the house and to keep the house together? Why or why not?
_____
_____

• What qualities did you need to exhibit in order to build the house?
_____
_____

• How do these qualities compare with the qualities needed to build and to keep together a domestic church?
_____
_____

Journal

The *Catechism of the Catholic Church* states, "Family life is an initiation into life in society" (#2207). Discuss how your family life has prepared you for life in society. For example, what lessons have you learned at home that have made it easier to get along with others?

Scripture Search

When a person finds out that he or she is going to be a parent, it is a time of joy and celebration. The Bible contains many stories of such blessed events. Read each of the following passages, filling in the chart as you read.

Scripture passage	Whose birth was announced?	How did the parents react?	What were the parents willing to do for their children?	How did the parents show love and respect for God?
Genesis 21:1–7, 22:1–19				
Exodus 1:1–22, 2:1–10				
Luke 1:26–55				

Parental duties

When a man and a woman marry, they must not only be willing to accept children, but they also must accept the responsibility to provide their children with a moral education and spiritual formation. Parents and guardians have the first responsibility for the education of their children. They first bear witness to this responsibility by creating a home where tenderness, forgiveness, respect, fidelity, and unselfish service are the rule. Those in the parental role have a serious responsibility to be good examples for their children.

Education in the faith by parents and guardians should begin in the child's earliest years. This already happens when family members help one another grow in faith by the witness of Christian lives that follow the example of Jesus. Parents and guardians also have the mission of teaching their children to pray and to discover their vocation as children of God. Through parental example, children must be convinced that the first vocation of the Christian is to follow Jesus.

Parents and guardians are dedicated to protecting and loving their children. Such dedication deserves honor and devotion. In addition, parents and guardians love and serve the Lord. They are to be the role models for how children should act as adult Christians.

Journal

What is one way in which your parents or guardians are a role model for you on how to act as an adult Christian?

_____
_____
_____
_____
_____
_____
_____
_____

Filial piety

Filial piety, or filial respect, refers to the respect that children have for their parents or guardians. This respect stems from gratitude toward the people who, by the gift of life, their love and their work, have brought children into the world. Filial respect helps create harmony in all of family life. Such respect means that when our parents or guardians ask us to help around the house, or to spend more time with the family, or to help take care of younger siblings, we should willingly obey. How many times have you answered your parents or guardians in a sarcastic or harsh tone when they have asked you to do something? Is that the way you would want to be treated?

Scripture Search

"With all your heart honor your father, and do not forget the birth pangs of your mother. Remember that it was of your parents you were born; how can you repay what they have given to you?" (Sirach 7:27–28)

Write a letter to your parents or guardians, thanking them for the gift of life. Tell them what you plan to give back to them as a sign of your gratitude for this gift. Write the draft of your letter here; transfer it to a sheet of paper when you are satisfied with the letter. Be sure to deliver the letter!

We are reminded of the Golden Rule that we discussed in chapter 1: "Do unto others as you would have them do unto you." We all want to be treated with love and respect. Your parents and guardians deserve to be answered in a loving, respectful tone. When they ask you to do something, it is because they value your help. They are bestowing responsibility upon you, and they trust that you can handle it. They are not trying to punish you by asking for your help. When they ask you to help out around the house, they are preparing you for the responsibility of having a house of your own someday. When they ask you to spend more time with the family, they are inviting you to learn more about what it means to be a member of a domestic church. When they ask you to help take care of younger siblings, they are instructing you for when you have a family of your own someday.

As you see, the domestic church really is a place where you learn your values and your morals. You learn to worship God. You learn to make good use of your freedom. You have guides who help you prepare for your future—and that's a good feeling!

THINK BEFORE YOU ACT

Many times we speak or we act without thinking. The following are some common scenarios. After reading each situation, write down what you think your immediate reaction to your parent(s) or guardian(s) might be. Then, after thinking about it, write down what you think you should do in each situation. Be as honest as you can in your answers.

Situation	Immediate reaction	Appropriate reaction
Your mom or dad asks you to help them with a project around the house; you are on the way out the door to meet your friends.		
Your mom or dad comments that you have been spending too much time with your friends and not enough time with your family.		
You have plans to go to a movie on Saturday night. Your parents want to go out that night, and they ask you to stay home and take care of your little brother or sister.		

How do your immediate reactions compare with the appropriate reactions? What can you do to be more respectful of your parents?

Sometimes we fall

Sometimes we fail to do what our parents or guardians ask us to do. We make mistakes, and we are punished. If you choose to go meet your friends instead of helping your mom or dad around the house, you might be punished. If you choose to spend more time with your friends than with your family, you might be punished. If you choose to go to a movie instead of taking care of your younger brother or sister, you might be punished.

Why do your parents or guardians punish you? No, it is not to hurt you or to make you suffer. Believe it or not, it is because they love you. When your parents or guardians correct you, they are only trying to help you be the best person that you can be. Your parents or guardians are trying to guide you on your way to being a loving, responsible adult. They only want what is best for you.

Once again, we are reminded that we should think before we speak or act. How we handle correction and criticism says a lot about who we are as children of God. Proverbs 13:1 states, "A wise child loves discipline, but a scoffer does not listen to rebuke."

Our parents or guardians have a great deal to offer. If you want to be a wise person, pay attention to them. Do as they ask. Be accepting of correction. When you need advice, ask your parents or guardians. They will be more than willing to help you. And so, you should be more than willing to help them.

Journal

How do you react when you are punished? Are you spiteful toward your parents or guardians? Do you run to your room and shut the door? Do you refuse to talk to them? Answer the questions below.

When was the last time that you were punished?
_____
_____

Who punished you?
_____
_____

What had you done?
_____
_____

What was your punishment?
_____
_____

How did you react?
_____
_____

How should you have reacted?
_____
_____

"CAPTAIN, MAY I?"

Select one student from the class to step forward and be the "captain." The captain, or the leader, stands at the front of the class. The rest of the class stands, too. The captain will give a direction to a member of the class, such as, "Chris, raise your right arm." Before raising his or her right hand, Chris must ask, "Captain, may I?" The captain then responds, "Yes, you may" (in which case Chris raises his or her right arm until instructed to do otherwise), or the captain responds, "No, you may not" (in which case Chris just stands there as before). Continue until everyone has gotten a chance to receive a direction. After the game, be prepared to answer the following questions:

Did you find it easy to obey? Why or why not?

_____
_____
_____
_____

What are some things that make it difficult to obey?

_____
_____
_____
_____

Why is it important to obey sometimes?

_____
_____
_____
_____

Called to obey

Because we are all servants of God, we are asked to work together. We are asked to work with God, our parents, our elders, our teachers, our employers—everyone. The fourth commandment incorporates all of these relationships. Since it deals with relationships beyond parents and children, you may be wondering why the commandment says "Honor your father and your mother." It is worded this way because the relationship between parents and children is one of the most universal.

In Luke 8:19–21, Jesus' mother and brothers come to visit him, and they are unable to get close to him. They wait outside as the crowd clears, and when Jesus is told that his mother and his brothers are waiting to see him, Jesus replies, "My mother and brothers are those who hear the word of God and obey it." Jesus did not mean any disrespect toward his mother and his brothers. He was making the point that we are all part of God's family, and we are called to love one another, not just the members of our domestic church.

Side Note

During the time of the Hebrew people, a child who hit or cursed at his or her parents was put to death. Similar to blasphemy and to not honoring the Sabbath, such actions were crimes against God and against human life.

Spiritual and temporal fruits

Obeying the fourth commandment brings its own rewards. Spiritual rewards refer to what is to come in the next life, such as eternal life. Temporal rewards refer to what is to take place in this life.

What are some ways in which you are good to your parents or guardians? If you are good to your parents or guardians in this life, what are some of the spiritual and temporal rewards?

FOLLOWING DIRECTIONS

It is not always easy to follow directions—and it is not always easy to give directions! Select a partner. One of you should sit in a desk facing the chalkboard; the other should sit in a desk facing away from the chalkboard. You will need paper and pencil. The teacher will draw a series of symbols or geographic designs on the chalkboard. The student who is facing the chalkboard should study the design on the chalkboard. He or she will then give verbal directions to instruct the other student how to draw what is on the chalkboard. No hand gestures—and no peeking! After you have finished, switch places and the teacher will draw a new design on the board. Then answer the following questions:

Was it easier to be the one giving directions or the one following directions? Why?

_____

_____

What does this tell you about what it is like to be a parent or guardian? A son or daughter?

_____

_____

How does this relate to the fourth commandment?

_____

_____

Scripture Search

Our duties to our parents or guardians are outlined throughout the Bible. Read Sirach 3:1–16. Describe Sirach's thoughts in your own words. What is it that Sirach is telling us to do? Describe how you are (or are not) doing these things in your own life.

Jesus gave honor to his Father

Jesus is the perfect example of a son who loved and respected his father. When God asked Jesus to do something, he did it. He was even willing to lay down his life! Your parents or guardians will probably never ask you to do anything as drastic as that, but Jesus serves as a model of how we are called to honor our mother and our father.

Whenever Jesus performed a miracle, or broke bread with friends, he gave honor and glory to the Father. Read the following passages that describe how Jesus loved and respected God.

- Matthew 14:13–21
- Mark 14:22–26
- Matthew 26:36–45

Notice how in each example Jesus reflected the words of the Lord's Prayer: "Give us this day our daily bread" and "Thy will be done." He always remembered to give thanks and praise to his Father in heaven. We should remember to do the same.

Being a positive reflection

We should also remember that our actions reflect on our parents or guardians. To a certain degree, our actions reveal what they have taught us. How closely do your actions reveal what your parents or guardians have taught you? When others look at you, do they see a person who was taught to love, honor, and obey?

You should strive to be a tribute to your parents or guardians. They have worked hard to provide for you. In turn, you should work hard to be a positive reflection of their work and teachings.

Eventually, you will be choosing your own vocation in life; you will decide "what you want to be when you grow up." When you choose, select a path that reflects your faith, your morals, and your values. Remember, your first calling is to follow Jesus. Your parents or guardians are providing a strong background. It is up to you to make a responsible decision as to what you will do with that preparation.

Journal

Right now, what do you want to be or do when you grow up? Why?

_____
_____
_____
_____

How does this choice reflect your faith? Your morals? Your values?

_____
_____
_____
_____
_____

Others have led us astray

Sometimes, people try to lead you down the wrong path. We have discussed how you already have a good idea of the difference between right and wrong, but it is not always so clear-cut. At times, the majority of the people around us are making wrong choices. They are forgetting that good is to be done and evil is to be avoided. We need to be reminded of the saying, "What is popular is not always right; what is right is not always popular."

For example, imagine that you are at a party. Someone approaches you with alcohol and says, "Everyone is doing it." How do you respond? You know what is right. You know what your parents or guardians have taught you. What do you do?

In Acts 5:29, Peter tells us, "We must obey God, rather than human authority." The fourth commandment reminds us that the majority is not always correct. Remember the Holocaust. Think of all of the German soldiers who committed horrible crimes against humanity in the concentration camps. When they were questioned about their acts, they all responded, "I am not responsible." They all said that they were "just following orders." The fourth commandment challenges us to remember that we only have one set of orders to follow: God's orders. If someone asks us to do something that is against God's orders—even if that person is a parent or guardian—then we have the right and the duty to obey God, not human beings.

Scripture Search

Read the following proverbs that deal with parent/child relationships:

- Proverbs 1:8
- Proverbs 17:25
- Proverbs 22:6
- Proverbs 23:24–25

In small groups, write three original proverbs that you believe are necessary to create good relationships between parents or guardians and children.

Pause to Pray

Dear Lord,
As we pray, we remember the words that Elizabeth spoke to Mary at the announcement of Jesus' birth: "You are the most blessed of all women, and blessed is the child you will bear!" Help us be children who are a blessing, and not a burden, to our parents or guardians. Help us honor and obey them, just as Jesus honored and obeyed you.
Amen.

Journal

What does it mean to be a "good" son or daughter? How do you exhibit these qualities? What could you be doing to be a better son or daughter?

Homework

1. Look back at your homework from chapter 1. You were to read each of the Ten Commandments, then put each commandment into your own words. How did you phrase the fourth commandment? Now that you have completed chapter 4, is there anything that you would like to add? Take this time to record any changes below.

2. Think of ten rules (commandments) that a son or daughter would follow to show love and honor for his or her parents or guardians. You can discuss this with your parents or guardians to get even more ideas. You might want to brainstorm ideas in small groups. You want your commandments to outline specific attitudes and behaviors. When you have decided upon your ten commandments, draw stone tablets on butcher paper or construction paper. On these tablets, write your commandments. Display them in your classroom as a daily reminder of how we are called to love and to honor our parents or guardians.

Chapter 5
You Shall Not Kill

In a small group, finish the following statement with four appropriate responses.

To be pro-life means . . .

Share your responses with the class.

Human life is sacred

"You shall not murder" (Exodus 20:13). The fifth commandment upholds the sacredness of human life. All life is the creative action of God. God alone is the Lord of life from its beginning until its end; no one under any circumstance can directly claim the right to destroy an innocent human being. This chapter centers on issues dealing with the sacredness of life that our Church constantly needs to address and defend.

Scripture specifies the prohibition of killing contained in the fifth commandment: "Keep far from a false charge, and do not kill the innocent and those in the right, for I will not acquit the guilty" (Exodus 23:7). The direct or indirect murder of an innocent person is gravely contrary to the dignity of the human being, to the Golden Rule, and to the holiness of the Creator. The law forbidding it is universally valid; it obliges each and everyone, always and everywhere.

SELF-DEFENSE

Discuss with your classmates whether or not you feel it is right to use self-defense that could ultimately kill your aggressor. When finished, ask your teacher to read the Church's position on this issue from the *Catechism of the Catholic Church* (#s 2263–67).

Abortion

While it is true that from dust we came and to dust we shall return, God is the only one who has the right to give life—or to take it away. Since the first century, the Church has affirmed the moral evil of every procured abortion. This teaching has not changed and remains unchangeable.

Catechism Clip

Human life must be respected and protected absolutely from the moment of conception. From the first moment of his existence, a human being must be recognized as having the rights of a person—among which is the inviolable right of every innocent being to life. [Cf. CDF, Donum vitae *I, 1.] (#2270)*

What science tells us and what the Church teaches is that at the moment of conception, when the DNA from the father's sperm unites with the DNA from the mother's egg, all the qualities of a new, unique human person are present: gender, hair, eye and skin color, facial features, size at adulthood, even intelligence and certain emotional traits. The fertilized egg continues to develop for the next nine months according to the instructions received at conception. The Church teaches that everything the new person will be at birth is already present in that fertilized egg. Destroying that fertilized egg at any stage in its development prior to birth is similar to destroying the baby at birth. The effect is ultimately the same—a human being is killed. Therefore, abortion is wrong according to the fifth commandment.

For the Hebrew people, the crime of murder carried with it the death penalty. It was considered to be a crime against God and against human nature. In today's Church, abortion is considered to be a "criminal" penalty. For today's Catholics, the penalty for formal cooperation in an abortion is excommunication, since it is a crime against human life.

Side Note

Excommunication is the penalty imposed by the Church for grave sins. Excommunication means that an individual is no longer able to receive the sacraments. Absolution of such a sin can only be granted by the pope, a bishop, or a priest authorized by one of these two. This is the most severe penalty that the Church can impart upon a member.

Journal

What are your personal feelings about abortion?

_____
_____
_____
_____
_____
_____
_____
_____

The gift of life

All people are responsible for the life given to them by God, who remains Master of all life. We are obliged to accept life gratefully and preserve it for God's honor and the salvation of our souls. God has entrusted this life to us; we are not free to dispose of it.

Suicide contradicts one's acceptance of the gift of life. It is seriously contrary to love of self and of love for the living God. Life is to be cherished. The taking of one's own life also offends love of neighbor because it unjustly severs ties with family and community.

Locate a photograph of yourself and tape or paste it in the center of an 8½" x 11" sheet of paper. Using words, phrases, or symbols, surround your photo with as many reasons as you can on why you cherish the gift of life. Be prepared to share your work with the class, and then post the paper somewhere as a reminder of your acceptance of the gift of life.

Catechism Clip

The use of drugs *inflicts very grave damage on human health and life. Their use, except on strictly therapeutic grounds, is a grave offense....* (#2291)

MERCY?

Euthanasia (often called "mercy killing") is the act or practice of killing or permitting the death of hopelessly sick or injured individuals in a relatively painless way for reasons of mercy.

Euthanasia has been a highly-debated topic in the news as of late. Many states are establishing laws that outlaw assisted suicide. In small groups, do some research to find out what the laws are in your state surrounding assisted suicide. Look into the ethical issues surrounding the topic of assisted suicide, and then report your findings to the class.

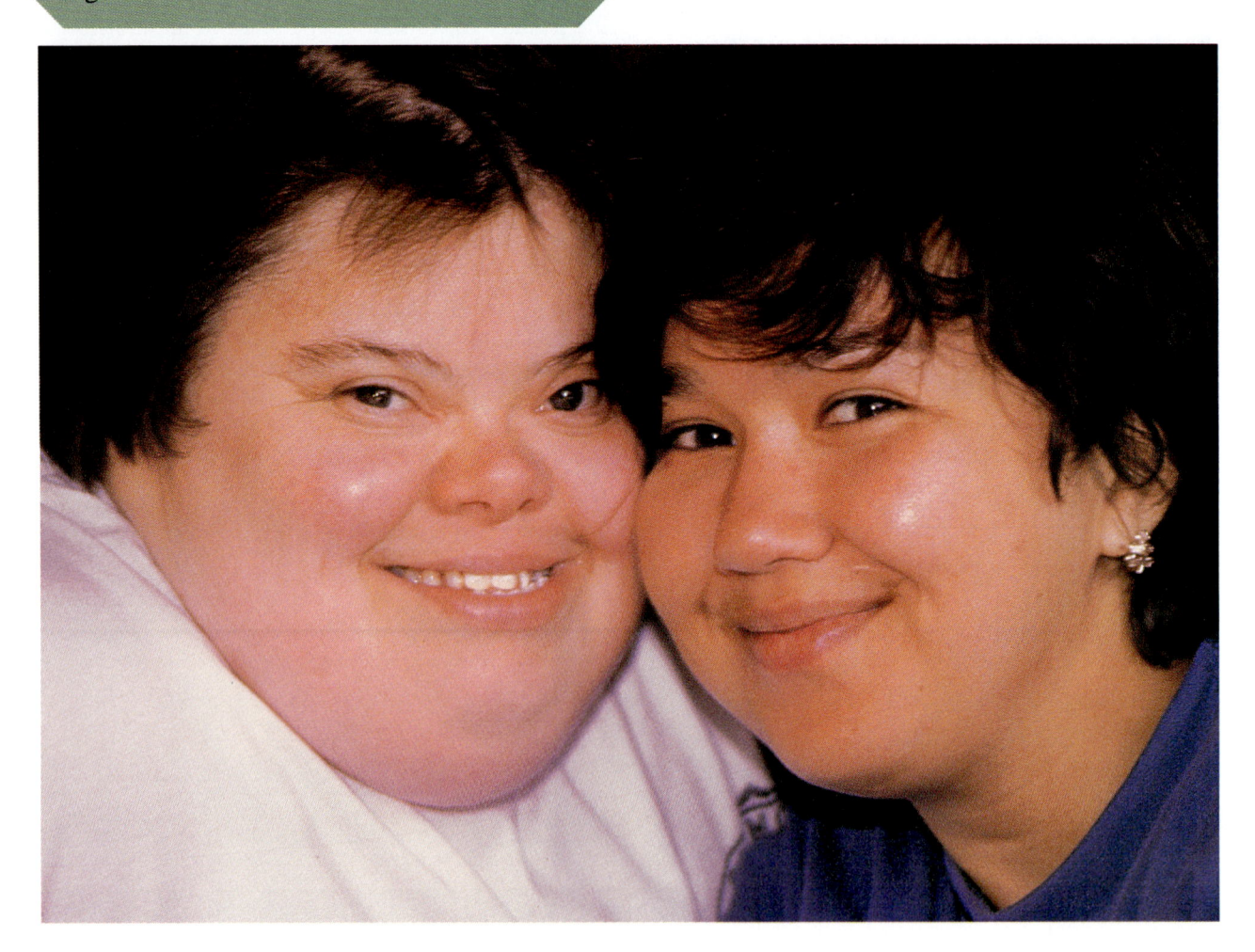

Catechism Clip

Whatever its motives and means, direct euthanasia consists in putting an end to the lives of handicapped, sick, or dying persons. It is morally unacceptable. (#2277)

❌ CAST YOUR VOTE ❌

The following statements reflect issues in the news these days. How do you feel about these statements? Circle your choice and give the reason(s) for your decisions.

1. Eliminate the death penalty.

   Agree   **Disagree**

   Why? _____
   _____
   _____

2. Tighten gun control laws so fewer people can own handguns and automatic weapons.

   Agree   **Disagree**

   Why? _____
   _____
   _____

3. Eliminate nuclear weapons in the United States.

   Agree   **Disagree**

   Why? _____
   _____
   _____

4. Require all students to go through metal detectors before entering the school building.

   Agree   **Disagree**

   Why? _____
   _____
   _____

5. Make private paramilitary groups illegal.

   Agree   **Disagree**

   Why? _____
   _____
   _____

6. Pass laws restricting the amount of violence shown on TV and in movies.

   Agree   **Disagree**

   Why? _____
   _____
   _____

Compare your choices with those of your classmates. Discuss your reasons.

Carte blanche

In chapter 1, we discussed how as you grow, you gain an increased understanding of who you are as a person. You are realizing that being free to be your own person does not mean that you are free to do whatever you want. Being your own person does not grant you carte blanche—the ability to do whatever you want with little or no regard for others. Part of being who you are involves being mindful and respectful of others.

The Church has a lot to teach about making responsible decisions. Become familiar with the Church's social teachings. Use your knowledge to recognize injustices. By so acting, we are signs of the kingdom of God among us. At the end of time, we will be judged on love.

There are signs that, with our free will, we can make decisions that are unselfish and positive. We can all help out, in some way. You know the Church's moral teachings, your talents, the amount of time you have, and the issue most important to you.

Journal

When was the last time that you encountered violence?

What was the situation?

What did you do?

Were you involved?

If so, were you the victim or the instigator?

How did you feel?

Violence all around

How many times in one day do you encounter violence? Hopefully, you do not experience violence personally on a daily basis, but you may *encounter* violence. Violence is all around us. It is on the television, on the radio, in your neighborhood.

Side Note

By the time that you are eighteen, you will probably have witnessed over 100,000 killings on TV shows and in the movies.

The practice of nonviolence

In regard to the fifth commandment, God calls us to practice nonviolence. To help gain an understanding of the Bible's teachings about nonviolence, read the following passages. Match each passage with what it teaches about nonviolence.

___ Matthew 5:22   A. teaching about anger

___ Matthew 5:39   B. teaching about revenge

___ Matthew 26:52   C. teaching about violence

As you can see, the fifth commandment not only instructs us not to kill, but it also warns us against being angry with each other, taking revenge on someone who wrongs us, and living by the sword. While the Old Testament taught us an eye for an eye, a tooth for a tooth, the New Testament challenges us to love one another.

Peter asked Jesus, "Lord, if my brother keeps on sinning against me, how many times do I have to forgive him? Seven times?" To which Jesus replied, "No, not seven times, but seven times seventy times" (Matthew 18:21–22). Unless we forgive one another in our hearts, those sins that are held bound on earth will be held bound in heaven. An end to violence will only become reality when forgiveness and love become the focus of all people's lives.

Journal

Imagine you are the elected leader of a country. What steps would you take that you feel could lead to greater world peace?

PEACE COLLAGE

As you look through newspapers and magazines today, it is very easy to find pictures and articles about violence. Here is your challenge: search through newspapers and magazines to find pictures and articles showing people who are practicing peace, not violence, love, not hate. Cut out these pictures and articles and make a collage by gluing them onto a piece of cardboard. You may want to cut your cardboard into the shape of a heart or a peace sign to help bring your images to life. When you are finished, display the collage in your classroom.

Institutional violence

Institutional violence involves a group in power who attempts to legitimize violence against an individual or a group. People who believe in institutional violence are the type of people who do not forgive one another in their hearts. They hold grudges. They seem unable to let go of the past.

Capital punishment

Although capital punishment is legal in many states, it is a form of institutional violence. While it has been in existence for centuries, capital punishment involves destruction by the system. It is an action of anger and hatred. It is often supported by people who are unable to forgive in their hearts. They rely heavily on one Old Testament teaching of an eye for an eye, and they forget that Jesus taught us to forgive one another.

Political prisoners

The fifth commandment tells us that it is not enough to avoid killing. We must also stand up against social injustices. While you may not know any political prisoners personally, you know that it is wrong to torture them. In our world today, we see the horrors that are taking place around the world, in such places as Bosnia. On television, millions of people see these innocent people being tortured every day. Yet what do we do about it? Organizations such as Amnesty International help fight injustices against political prisoners.

Police brutality

With the addition of video cameras to police cars, we are seeing more and more instances of police brutality. While these cameras were originally installed to help protect the police officer (in case something went wrong during an arrest), they have come to reveal a very serious problem in our society. The issue of police brutality was brought to the forefront during the Rodney King trial, when an African American male was severely beaten by California police officers. People around the world were outraged by this display of anger and hatred. Again, what do we do about it? It is not enough to avoid killing. As Christians, we are challenged to stand up against injustices.

The riots that ensued following the Rodney King trial were not an answer to the problem, either. Violence begets violence, and we need to avoid the "mob mentality" of anger and hatred.

Gang violence

Gang violence is on the rise around our country today. It is another example of how violence begets violence. If one gang does something to harm the members of another gang, then the violence only escalates.

Are you aware of any gang activity in your community? Are you familiar with any gang symbols? If so, which ones? Where do you see them, and how did you come to know what they mean? How does your community work to prevent or combat gang violence?

PUTTING WORDS INTO ACTION

As a class, separate into three groups. Each group will represent one facet of violence. One group will be assigned to represent political prisoners, a second group police brutality, and a third, gang violence. In your group, put together a skit—involving everyone—that shows how your behavior is a problem in our society today. Then, as a group, come up with a way to resolve the problem. Share your skit with your classmates. After each skit, stop and talk about the behavior presented and how it affects your life and your world today.

CURRENT EVENTS

Form groups of four. Each of the following topics is hotly debated in communities around the country. In your small groups, select one of the following topics to research. Two of you will research the pro side of the issue; two of you will research the con side of the issue. You can use newspapers, magazines, personal interviews, or any other sources. Find out as much as you can about your topic, being certain to gain an understanding of your assigned side of the issue. (Keep in mind that you may not personally agree with your assigned stance.) Then, in your small groups, organize a mock debate. Have each pair present their side of the issue to the class. At the end, see if anyone has persuaded another's beliefs on the issue.

Topics:

- The death penalty
- Assisted suicide
- Gun control
- Violence on TV and in the movies
- Gang acctivity
- Violence in schools

All life is sacred

As you can see, the main principle of this commandment is clear enough: All life is sacred. God, as author of all life, has the ultimate authority over all life. The fifth commandment instructs us to respect and care for all life, human and otherwise, our own and that of others. The commandment applies to us as individuals. It applies to society and governments, too.

On the personal level, the fifth commandment primarily calls you to "clean living," to shunning violence in all its forms. On both the personal and government levels, it forbids practices like suicide, abortion, and euthanasia. Even if a government "legalizes" these practices, they are still wrong.

Finally, if you want an example of what this commandment really means and looks like in practice, you'll find it on almost every page of the Gospels. Jesus shunned all forms of violence. He forgave rather than attacked his enemies, even though it cost him his life. He continually sought to heal and restore health. He loved and called the people's attention to the beauty and wonder of nature.

Jesus teaches his disciples to be meek, merciful peacemakers, nonviolent persons. That is the direct opposite of the trend in our society, which glorifies being tough and macho, getting even, using the might-makes-right approach to solving differences. Jesus has personally called you to be one of his disciples. That's a real honor. But going against social trends is also a real challenge. Is someone your age up to the challenge? Jesus thinks so.

Side Note

Catholics are called to have a "consistent ethic of life." Based on our belief that all life is sacred and that taking even one human life is a momentous event, this ethic means Catholics are to believe that all murder is gravely wrong. It is not consistent to be against abortion and yet support capital punishment. Life is to be held sacred at all times and in all circumstances. Do you have a consistent ethic of life?

Where do we go from there?

We are made in God's image, and we should be raised in God's image. After we are born, we are raised in a domestic church, as discussed in chapter 4. As members of a family, we develop our faith, our morals, and our values. As part of our Christian upbringing, we are taught to honor the Great Commandment and the Beatitudes.

The Great Commandment

We have discussed the greatest commandment: "Love the Lord your God with all your heart, with all your soul, and with all your mind." We also know that the second most important commandment is like it: "Love your neighbor as you love yourself." If we are truly loving, then we have no room in our hearts to hold grudges or to harm another person. We should devote our energies to loving the Lord, not hating our neighbor.

The Beatitudes

In chapter 1, we discussed how the Beatitudes help guide us to true happiness. They reiterate the greatest commandment of all: We are called to love God and to love one another. In loving God and in loving each other, we find true happiness. The Ten Commandments and the Beatitudes supply directions for how to love and how to serve one another. If we are indeed willing to do what God requires, if we are indeed willing to be merciful, and if we indeed work for peace, then the fifth commandment will not be a problem to follow. Review the Beatitudes by reading Matthew 5:1–12.

Scripture Search

Separate into five groups. Each group should be assigned one of the following Scripture passages. As a group, read the passage aloud. Summarize what it means and discuss how it applies in everyday life. Share your insights with the class.

Scripture passage	Summary	How it applies to my life
Matthew 5:21–26		
Matthew 5:38–42		
Matthew 5:43–48		
Matthew 7:1–5		
Matthew 7:7–12		

Pause to Pray

*God, thank you for your great love
and all that you give to me.
Give me the grace and the courage
to live a life of nonviolence
so that I may be faithful to Jesus.
Send me your spirit that I may love everyone
as my sister and my brother and not fear anyone.
Help me to be an instrument of your peace;
to respond with love
and not to retaliate with violence;
to accept suffering rather than inflict it;
to live more simply;
to resist death and to choose life
for all your children.
Guide me along the way of nonviolence.
Disarm my heart
and I shall be your instrument
to disarm other hearts.
Lead me, God of nonviolence,
into your reign of love and peace,
where there is no fear and no violence.
In the name of Jesus. Amen.*

—from **The Fire of Peace**, written by John Dear SJ

Journal

Do you consider yourself to be pro-life? Give examples of your beliefs.

Are you a peacemaker? If someone does something against you, are you quick to forgive, or do you hold a grudge? What do you do to promote peace in your own life?

Homework

1. Look back at your homework from chapter 1. You were to read each of the Ten Commandments, then put each commandment into your own words. How did you phrase the fifth commandment? Now that you have completed chapter 5, is there anything that you would like to add? Take this time to record any changes here in your textbook.

2. Imagine that one of your peers is struggling to cherish the gift of life, even hinting about the possibility of suicide. In addition to alerting responsible adults to the situation, write a letter to your peer. Share why you feel the gift of life is so precious. Be prepared to share your letter in class.

   Dear _____ ,

   My prayers are with you.

   _____

Chapter 6
You Shall Not Commit Adultery
You Shall Not Covet Your Neighbor's Wife

INTERVIEW

Interview a married couple, asking them to answer the following list of questions. Write down their responses. You will be asked to share several of their thoughts with the class.

• When were you married?

• What stands out most about your wedding day?

• What do you feel are the three most important characteristics in a marriage?

• What do you cherish most about your spouse?

• What advice would you give to others about marriage?

Love and faithfulness

"You shall not commit adultery" (Exodus 20:14).

"You shall not covet your neighbor's house; you shall not covet your neighbor's wife, or male or female slave, or ox, or donkey, or anything that belongs to your neighbor" (Exodus 20:17).

Both the sixth and ninth commandments deal with love and faithfulness. They incorporate the responsibilities surrounding your human sexuality. Through the mature and ethical use of your sexuality, you are able to become a life-giving partner with God. Both of these commandments call you to respect this life-giving capacity by using it responsibly in a loving, faithful marriage. In this chapter, we will be exploring what all this entails.

Before going any further, we should discuss the terms *adultery* and *covet. Adultery* is when a married person voluntarily takes part in sexual relations and/or intercourse with someone other than his or her lawful spouse. To *covet* is to wrongfully desire what someone else has.

God must think that marriage and the responsibilities of parenting are very important. After all, he devotes two of the ten commandments to warning against the infidelity that can destroy marriage. To emphasize the point, God gave us one commandment that opposes the physical act of entering into a sexual relationship that adulterates a faithful marriage (the sixth commandment), and then another commandment that opposes even thinking about or desiring to do so (the ninth commandment). Both of these commandments seek to preserve and to protect marriage itself.

Scripture Search

Take a moment to read Matthew 5:27–32. This passage illustrates how your thoughts, words, and actions can prevent you from being a loving, faithful follower of Christ. What do you think about what Jesus has to say?

In God's image

We are created, male and female, in God's image. God has blessed us and has called us to be fruitful and multiply. Our sexuality is a part of this. It binds our heart and our soul, and it allows us to form meaningful bonds with others. You should acknowledge and accept your sexual identity. It is nothing to be embarrassed about; it is a gift from God.

A PRECIOUS GIFT

What is the most precious gift that you can think of? What makes it precious? In the space below, draw a picture of this precious gift.

Your sexuality is also a precious gift. God allows for us to share this gift with our spouse in the bonds of matrimony. As it says in Genesis 2:24, "A man leaves his father and mother and is united with his wife, and they become one." The full expression of your sexuality is to be reserved for marriage.

Taking charge

Chastity is the state or quality of remaining chaste, meaning that you refrain from taking part in unlawful (or nonmarital) sexual intercourse. All Christ's faithful are called to lead a chaste life in keeping with their particular states in life: if married, only having sexual relations with your spouse; if single, reserving sexual intercourse for marriage; if celibate, abstaining from all sexual relations.

As a single member of Christ's faithful, you must refuse to take part in premarital sex. For people your age, there can indeed be a lot of pressure to take part in premarital sex. If you are a person of integrity who respects your body, then you will resist this temptation and reserve sexual intercourse for marriage.

Chastity calls for self-mastery. As we discussed earlier, God has entrusted us with free will. It is up to us to make the right decisions and to take charge of our own lives. The *Catechism of the Catholic Church* instructs us that "the alternative is clear: either man governs his passions and finds peace, or he lets himself be dominated by them and becomes unhappy" (#2339). You know what is right; the choice is yours. Respect yourself and choose to save the precious gift of your sexuality for marriage.

Journal

How does the media challenge the value of chastity?
_____
_____
_____

Along with the concept of free will in decision making comes self-control and self-restraint. It is similar to when you come home from school and see that your mom has baked a cake for supper. You might be really hungry, but you know that your mom wants to save the cake until after the whole family has eaten. You resist the urge to eat some of the cake because you don't want to disappoint your mom—and yourself. With your sexuality, you must also strive to control the urge to take part in premarital sex. You don't want to disappoint God—or yourself. You are a person of integrity and self-control.

Journal

Who is one of your good friends? What qualities make this friendship special?
_____
_____
_____
_____
_____
_____
_____
_____
_____

Developing friendships

You are in the process of growing up and becoming your own person. You are developing friendships with both boys and girls. Friendship is a form of spiritual unity. Jesus had many friends, of both sexes. He showed us that friendship is an important part of life. Through loving and befriending others, we show our love for and friendship with God.

Scripture Search

For each of the following Scripture passages, write down the specific name(s) of Jesus' friend(s) who are mentioned.

Matthew 15:13–20 _____

Mark 32:32–34 _____

Luke 10:38–41 _____

John 11:1–5 _____

As you grow, certain friendships may lead to deeper relationships. You may meet someone who shares the same values, morals, and beliefs that you do. In addition, you should share mutual respect. With time you may decide to get married. Like being single or choosing a celibate lifestyle, marriage is a calling—or vocation—in life.

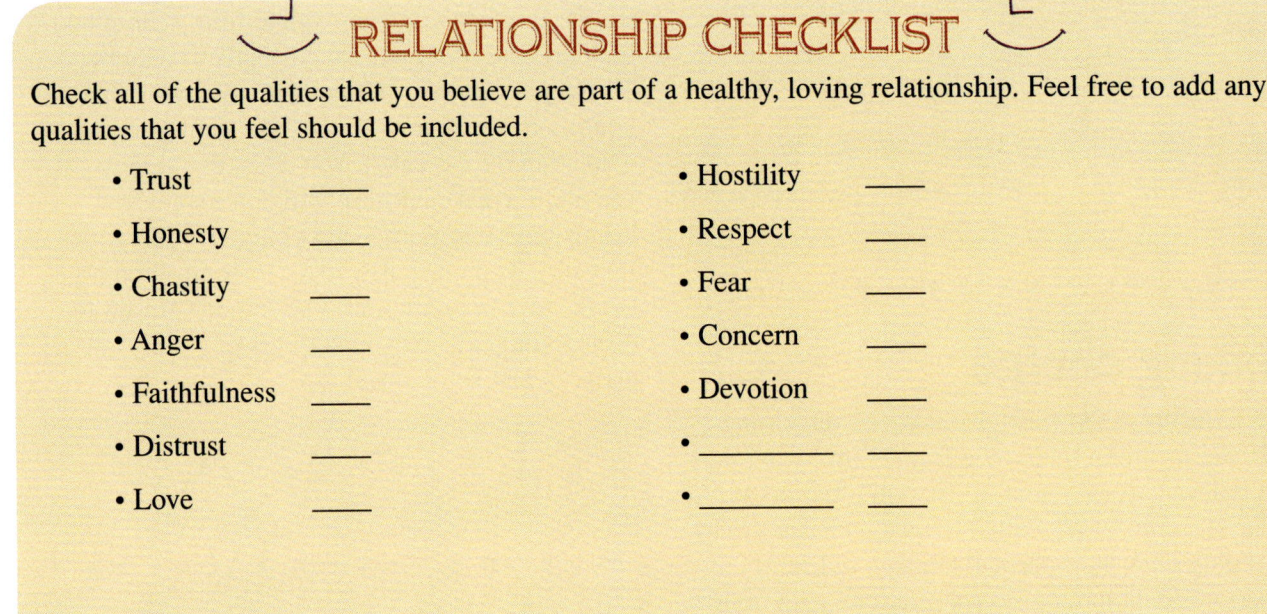

RELATIONSHIP CHECKLIST

Check all of the qualities that you believe are part of a healthy, loving relationship. Feel free to add any qualities that you feel should be included.

- Trust   ____
- Honesty   ____
- Chastity   ____
- Anger   ____
- Faithfulness   ____
- Distrust   ____
- Love   ____

- Hostility   ____
- Respect   ____
- Fear   ____
- Concern   ____
- Devotion   ____
- _____   ____
- _____   ____

Discuss your answers with your classmates. Make careful note of those qualities that you consider to be part of a healthy, loving relationship. Settle for nothing less than what you deserve. In turn, be sure that you express these qualities to those you love.

Be aware

Now that we have discussed the principles of chastity, we need to discuss those things that work against chastity. Certain actions can harm our relationships with God, with others, and with ourselves. We need to know what they are so that we can avoid falling into their traps.

1. *Lust* is strong and disordered desire for another human being. Any time that you dehumanize a person to the state of object, you are showing disrespect for that person.

2. *Masturbation* is "the deliberate stimulation of the sexual organs in order to achieve sexual pleasure." This is harmful because it involves the use of sexual organs for purposes other than their procreative purpose.

3. *Fornication* involves the sexual union between an unmarried man and an unmarried woman. Since sexual intercourse is to be reserved for those who are married, fornication shows a lack of respect for those individuals involved.

4. *Pornography* consists of highy-sexual materials that are considered evil because they remove sexual acts from the intimacy of the partners involved. It exhibits disrespect for everyone involved. It takes away the sanctity of the intimate giving of spouses to one another, and it should be avoided.

5. *Prostitution* reduces a person to an instrument of sexual pleasure and money. A person's body is a temple, and such acts violate the temple of the Holy Spirit.

6. *Rape* is forcing sexual intimacy onto another person. Rape violates the victim's respect, freedom, and integrity—and no one has the right to do that to another human being.

WHAT CAN BE DONE?

In small groups, select one of the topics listed on page 67. Discuss what you think causes the problem in our society today. Where do you see examples of the problem? Brainstorm ideas about what can be done to solve or to prevent the problem. You can use the space below to keep track of your thoughts. Present your ideas to your classmates.

What causes the problem?	Where do you see examples?	What can be done?

To love, honor, and cherish

In marriage, a man and a woman promise to love, honor, and cherish one another. In doing so, they show respect for each other. In a respectful relationship, physical intimacy between spouses becomes a sign and a pledge of their spiritual communion.

Physical intimacy in marriage serves two purposes. First of all, it provides for the good of the spouses. The union allows the husband and wife the opportunity to show their love for one another through love and faithfulness. Secondly, it allows for the transmission of life. The union allows for the opportunity for the couple to have children, which is a true blessing.

Marriage is an intimate partnership of love and life. It is a covenant between two people who agree to love, honor, and cherish one another. Both partners give themselves freely and completely. As stated in Mark 10:9, "Man must not separate, then, what God has joined together."

MARRIAGE SURVEY

Think about some of the weddings that you have attended. What symbols are present that express the couple's devotion to one another? In small groups, make a collage of the symbols of loving, honoring, and cherishing one another. Include any pictures that show how marriage is a partnership, a joining together. Share your collage with your classmates, then post it somewhere in the classroom as a reminder of the significance of the union of marriage.

A special gift

Fecundity, or childbearing, is a gift of marriage. Married couples are called to be open to this gift. As the *Catechism of the Catholic Church* expresses it, "A child does not come from outside as something added on to the mutual love of the spouses, but springs from the very heart of that mutual giving, as its fruit and fulfillment" (#2366). In doing so, married couples are allowed to take part in the procreative and parenthood role of God. What a gift!

While a couple may wish to space out their children, they should make sure that such a choice is made responsibly, not selfishly. The Church sees large families as a sign of God's blessing, yet it is understandable that parents would want to be able to give the proper care to each child.

There seems to be a growing number of married couples who, for one reason or another, are unable to have children. Science is sometimes capable of solving their problems, but in many cases, the interventions used to promote conception are contrary to the Church's teaching on the responsible use of our sexuality. In situations where the husband is infertile, the wife may choose to become pregnant by having her egg artificially fertilized in a test tube, using the sperm of a man other than her husband.

In cases where the wife is incapable of becoming pregnant, some couples resort to what is called a *surrogate mother*. The husband impregnates another woman, artificially or naturally, and this woman agrees to give up the baby to the couple upon birth.

Even if no intercourse is involved, *all* this is technically a kind of adultery, and therefore is forbidden by the Church. Even though the intentions are admirable and the couple is most eager to use their sexuality to bring forth new life, these artificial or "third party" approaches are in contradiction to the nature of marriage and the responsible use of sexuality. Even when a third party is not involved, the Church opposes technological methods that separate reproduction from the natural act of sexual reproduction.

Though this may not have much practical meaning for you at this point in your life, it is important that you understand how science is affecting society's approach to human reproduction. It's also important that you stay in touch with the Church's teaching on the subject. While some scientific discoveries may be helping couples become parents while being sexually responsible, much of what scientific research and practice promote goes against God's plan for human sexuality. It is important for you to be able to differentiate between the two.

I AM A BLESSING!

You, too, are a blessing to your parents. When you were born, you were their little bundle of joy. Go home and look through a family photo album with your parents. Ask if you can bring in one of your baby pictures. (If you can't find a baby picture, see if you can find one of when you were a toddler.) Without revealing your identity to your classmates, make a bulletin board of everyone's baby pictures. See how many classmates you can correctly identify!

Until death do us part

Unfortunately, for various reasons, fewer and fewer couples are adhering to the "Until death do us part" aspect of their marriage vows. Divorce is on the rise in the United States. What is causing this? What is the Church's stand?

Side Note

The canon law of the Church acknowledges certain instances where the separation of spouses is legitimate. "If civil divorce remains the only possible way of ensuring certain legal rights, the care of the children, or the protection of inheritance, it can be tolerated and does not constitute a moral offense." Can you name such an instance?

Divorce, however, is a grave offense against natural law when a partner claims to marry a second partner. It breaks the covenant between a man and a woman who have been joined by God. Divorce is breaking a sacred promise, in fact, one of the biggest promises that can be made.

Journal

What is the biggest promise that you have ever made? Did you keep the promise? If you broke the promise, why did you do it? What were the consequences?

_____
_____
_____

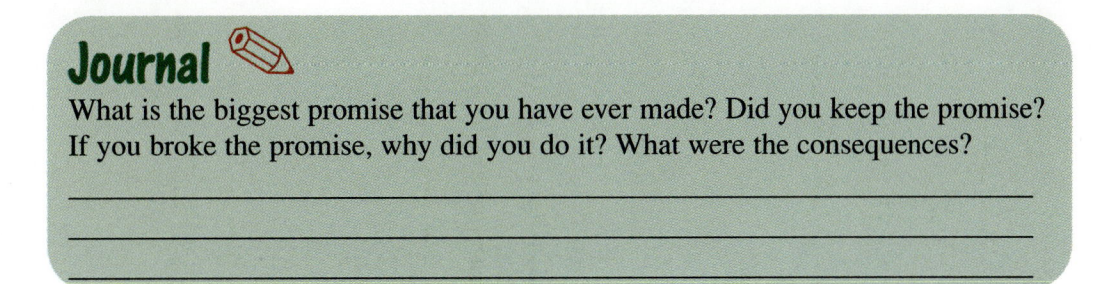

Scripture Search

Read the following Scripture passages. Summarize what each has to say about divorce.

• Malachi 2:13–16
_____
_____
_____

• Deuteronomy 24:1–4
_____
_____
_____

Pause to Pray

Dear Lord,
You extend a calling to many different vocations. Please help me answer my calling with love and faithfulness.
If I am called to be a single person,
then allow me to answer my calling by helping serve others and serve you.
If I am called to be a married person,
then allow me to answer my calling with love and fidelity.
If I am called to the religious life,
then allow me to serve you with my whole heart and my whole soul.
Whatever you have chosen for me, Lord, help open my ears to your calling.
Amen.

Journal

What do you feel are the greatest challenges for you to live a chaste lifestyle?

_____
_____
_____

Homework

1. Look back at your homework from chapter 1. You were to read each of the Ten Commandments, then put each commandment into your own words. How did you phrase the sixth and ninth commandments? Now that you have completed chapter 6, is there anything that you would like to add? Take this time to record any changes below.

2. Select a television show or a movie that deals with marriage. Watch the program, and then write a review explaining how the show dealt with the concepts of love and marriage discussed in this chapter. Include a personal reaction to the show.

    • Review

    • Reaction

Chapter 7

You Shall Not Steal
You Shall Not Covet Your Neighbor's Goods

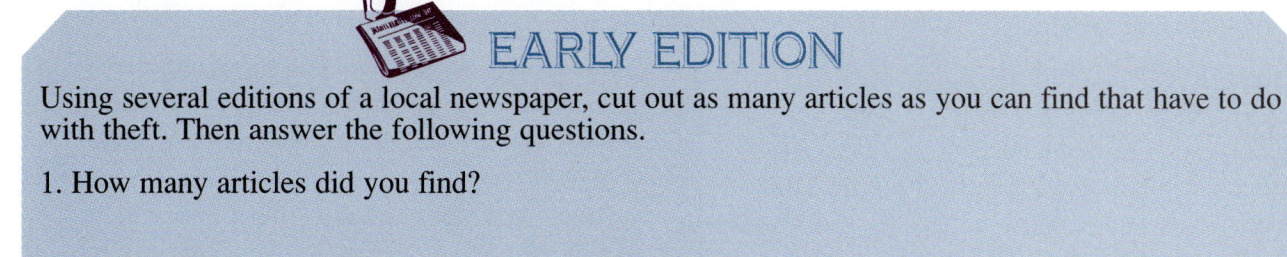

EARLY EDITION

Using several editions of a local newspaper, cut out as many articles as you can find that have to do with theft. Then answer the following questions.

1. How many articles did you find?

2. Does this number surprise you? Why or why not?

3. Why do you think the various items were stolen? Do you believe there could be different reasons for the different instances? Why?

4. How would you suggest your community combat theft?

Good advice

How many times have you heard your parents say, "Keep your hands to yourself" or "Don't touch anything"? Both of these comments instruct us to keep our hands off those things that do not belong to us. Pretty good advice, don't you think? These comments help us understand the seventh and tenth commandments.

Where your heart is

The seventh and tenth commandments speak to what it is that lies at the heart of people. The two command-ments call the faithful to stay focused on what is important in life and to the salvation of their souls. In the words of Jesus, "For where your treasure is, there your heart will be also" (Matthew 6:21).

The seventh commandment—*"You shall not steal"* (Exodus 20:15)—forbids us from unjustly taking or keeping anything that belongs to another person. It calls us to take care of our worldly possessions and to treat them responsibly. It calls us to respect others' right to private property. The tenth commandment—*"You shall not covet your neighbor's house; you shall not covet your neighbor's wife, or male or female slave, or ox, or donkey, or anything that belongs to your neighbor"* (Exodus 20:17)—forbids us from coveting, or desiring, anything that belongs to another person, as such desire is the root of theft, robbery, and fraud. It calls us to avoid *avarice*, the thirst for riches.

Journal
When was a time that you coveted something belonging to someone else? How did you deal with your feelings?

___

Side Note
Vandalism is a form of stealing. Over a billion dollars worth of property is destroyed each year in the United States due to vandalism.

Misplaced desire

In your life, what do you desire? What should you desire? Sometimes we lose sight of what our true goals are. We get caught up in materialistic ideas, and we forget that we are called to love one another. The tenth commandment reminds us to keep our focus.

While it seems natural to envy others and to want the things that we do not have, like stylish shoes or brand-name jeans, we must be careful not to covet, or desire, that which does not belong to us. For example, it is okay to want a new Starter® jacket, but it is not okay to take someone else's jacket. The proper thing to do is to work hard to earn money for your own jacket, not to deprive someone else of what is rightfully theirs. Envy is a capital or deadly sin. It can consume you and keep you from loving your neighbor as yourself.

How do you avoid such misplaced desire? As a baptized Christian, you should seek to help others, to be humble, and to live as Jesus did. It all comes back to true happiness. If you follow the Beatitudes, you will find true happiness. The *Catechism of the Catholic Church* reads, "The promise [of seeing God] surpasses all beatitude.... In Scripture, to see is to possess.... Whoever sees God has obtained all the goods of which he can conceive."

Journal
What are some of the "goods" in your life for which you are especially grateful?

A higher responsibility

We all have the right to private property—to own our own possessions. You have the right to own your stereo, or roller blades, or soccer pads. Yet we have to make sure that we don't get so focused on the "This is mine!" attitude that we forget that we have a higher responsibility. Not only do we have the responsibility of taking care of our own possessions, but we also have the responsibility of remembering that God gave the whole earth—and everything on it—to all of us. Does that mean that you have to share your stereo with everyone on earth? Not exactly. If you can use what you own to benefit others, however, that is part of your calling. For example, if your friend was having a party, and he wanted to have music at the party but he didn't own a stereo of his own, you could offer to bring yours along to the party. That way, everyone at the party is benefiting. See how it works?

Scripture Search

What is your reaction to the story of the widow who was poor in Luke 21:1–4?

When was a time when you gave all (money or something else) that you had?

Respect for Others

In regard to these commandments, there are certain virtues that help preserve respect for human dignity. They are:

1. *Temperance*, moderation that requires us to control and to limit our attachment to worldly goods and pleasures;
2. *Justice*, which calls us to preserve and to respect the rights of others, and to give them what they deserve; and
3. *Solidarity*, which directs us to obey the Golden Rule ("Do unto others as you would have them do unto you"), and which is in keeping with the generosity of the Lord.

By practicing all three of these virtues, we can show respect for others and for their possessions.

An aspect of showing respect for others demands that we avoid theft, the taking of another's possessions without his or her expressed permission. This can be as simple as borrowing your sister's jacket without asking, to something as complex as breaking into a house and taking someone's television. The only time that theft is acceptable is if it can be presumed that the person would give his or her consent. For example, if you had a fire in your backyard and you borrowed your neighbor's hose without asking in order to help put out the fire. It can be assumed that your neighbor would not mind you using his or her property to ensure the safety of others.

Journal ✏️
Can you name another instance in which it is possible that theft could be acceptable?
_____
_____
_____

The seventh commandment also addresses borrowing people's property, yet not returning what you have borrowed. Deliberately holding onto something that does not belong to you is wrong. Let's say that you borrow a friend's CD and promise to give it back the next time that you see him. The next time that you see him, however, he doesn't ask for it back. Instead of voluntarily returning the CD, you hold onto it, figuring that he doesn't miss it. This, too, is a form of theft. The CD belongs to your friend, and it should be returned to him in a timely manner. If you don't return it, you are taking advantage of your friend's generosity.

Journal ✏️
When was a time someone borrowed something and did not return it in a timely manner, or at all? How did you feel?
_____
_____
_____

This commandment also incorporates the concepts of promises and contracts. An honorable person keeps his or her promises and fulfills the terms of his or her contracts. If you promise to clean your room before you go to practice, then you should clean your room before you go to practice. If you sign a contract saying that you will refrain from using drugs and alcohol in order to be on the basketball team, then you have an even stronger obligation to refrain from using drugs and alcohol than you would otherwise.

I PROMISE . . .
Compose a promise between yourself and God that states how you are willing to uphold the seventh and tenth commandments. Write the promise in the space below and then decorate it as you please. Be ready to share your promise with the class.

Stewards of the earth
While the seventh commandment focuses on actions, the tenth commandment focuses on intentions. Both commandments address the irresponsibility of keeping more than you need, without sharing, as in the economic IQ quiz on page 77.

TEST YOUR ECONOMIC IQ

Circle what you consider to be the correct answer to each question:

1. How many people in the world are slowly starving to death?

   1 in 5   1 in 25   1 in 50   1 in 100   1 in 1000

2. How many people die each year of starvation or sicknesses directly related to malnutrition?

   100,000   500,000   1,000,000   5,000,000   15,000,000

3. How many people are born in the world's poorest countries each year?

   1,000,000   5,000,000   25,000,000   50,000,000   75,000,000

4. How much of the world's annual grain crop goes to feeding animals in the world's wealthy countries?

   5 percent   10 percent   15 percent   25 percent   33 percent

5. Approximately how many people in the world will die of hunger-related causes in the next hour (or while you are in this session)?

   10   50   100   500   1000

6. How many of the world's 5.7 billion people live in *absolute poverty*?

   1 million   10 million   50 million   100 million   over 1 billion

7. What percent of the food needed to feed the world population is actually being produced?

   10 percent   25 percent   50 pecent   75 percent   over 100 percent

8. How many people in the United States are living in poverty?

   1 in 10   1 in 25   1 in 50   1 in 100   1 in 1000

As Christians, we are called to be stewards of the earth. That means that it is our duty to take care of the people, the animals, and the environment around us. The main concept of the seventh and tenth commandments incorporates respect for human life, but the commandments extend to a second level, calling for us to respect *all* life. This means respect for animals and the environment as a whole.

As humans, God has given us a share in his authority over other life forms. While we are allowed to use resources for our own legitimate needs, such as food, clothing, and shelter, we are not allowed unlimited license, or carte blanche, as we discussed earlier in this book. For example, an Inuit who kills a seal for food and clothing is exercising a legitimate authority. If a company that hunts seals to the point of extinction in order to make a profit, it violates these two commandments.

You hear a lot today about the destruction of the rain forest, the pollution of lakes and rivers, the waste of natural resources, and the growing list of endangered species. You also hear a lot about the importance of recycling, conserving energy, and preventing littering. All of these efforts demonstrate respect for all life.

The good news is that most people are becoming informed and concerned about our environment today. The bad news is that we still have a long way to go to reestablish that respect and care for our world that God intends for us. Whatever you do to help protect and restore the environment shows respect for all life and, therefore, honors the seventh and tenth commandments. On the other hand, being careless and wasteful of our natural resources violates both of these commandments.

Journal

Have you ever left something of value to you outside overnight, even after your parents reminded you to bring it in? If so, did anything happen to it? How did you feel?

_____
_____
_____

FRUITS OF THE EARTH

What are some of the ways in which your family, school, and community are demonstrating the importance of recycling and conserving energy? List your ideas below.

Family

School

Community

As a class, brainstorm other possibilities. As a class project, you may want to put one of your ideas into practice.

78

HOW MUCH FOR THE WRAPPER?

Find at least one advertisement or actual example of an item that is over-packaged. This may consist of double and triple packaging, or excessive use of paper, plastic, or other disposable materials. Individually-packaged items within a larger container, glossy bows, flowery arrangements, and other items may be included.

In small groups of two to four people, examine the item or the advertisement and determine the following:

1. What purpose did the manufacturer have in designing the package?

2. Does the package add value? What kind of value?

3. Does the design, shape, color, or added features have a direct relationship to the product?

4. Can the contents of the container be purchased in a different form (for example, in bulk, large-size containers, in less elaborate packages)? If yes, what is the comparative cost of the item in a less excessively-packaged form?

5. Identify and describe ways in which the packaging of the item contributes to excessive waste that may need to be recycled or sent to the landfill.

6. How does the package affect a retailer? Does it take up unnecessary space, or does it prevent shoplifting?

List the packaging criteria you think the manufacturer used; then explain reasons why the manufacturer used this means for packaging the product. Determine whether or not you think the packaging is appropriate, and be prepared to explain why. Also brainstorm ideas of alternative methods that the manufacturer could use to reduce the amount of packaging.

How does this activity relate to the seventh and tenth commandments? Why is it important to pay attention to details such as the packaging of products?

—*Adapted from pages 89–91 of the Iowa Department of Education handbook* Iowa's Clean Sweep.

Scripture Search

As a class, read aloud the story of creation in Genesis 1:1–2:4. How does this story reaffirm how the faithful are to be stewards (caretakers) of the earth and all that fills it?

TOUGH DECISIONS

Let's take a minute to stop and think about the decisions that we are (or are not) willing to make. Our decisions express a lot about us and our willingness to be a steward, or caretaker, of the earth. Take a look at the following scenarios. Think carefully about each of your responses; then discuss your answers in small groups. Be prepared to explain why you answered as you did.

1. Are there people you envy enough to want to trade lives with them? Who are they?

2. For an all-expense-paid, one-week vacation anywhere in the world, would you be willing to kill a beautiful butterfly by pulling off its wings? What about stepping on a cockroach? Why does a beautiful creature merit more compassion than an ugly one?

3. Would you rather be given $10,000 for your own use or $100,000 to give anonymously to strangers? What if you could keep $1,000,000 or give away $20,000,000?

4. If you walked out of your house one morning and saw a bird with a broken wing huddled in some nearby bushes, what would you do?

5. Walking along an empty street, you notice a wallet. It contains $5,000 in cash but no name or address. What would you do? Would it alter your decision if inside you found the name, address, and picture of either a wealthy-looking young man or a frail-looking old woman?

Social justice

Perhaps you have seen the bumper stickers that read, "If you want peace, work for justice." What exactly is *justice*? It's a word we hear often, but may not take the time to think about. In short, *justice* is fair treatment. We all deserve fair treatment, don't we?

An honest day's work for an honest day's pay should be equivalent to equal pay for equal work, yet we know that people are not always treated fairly. In our society, the civil rights movement and the equal rights movement have been striving to ensure that all people, regardless of gender or race, receive the same wages for the same work.

Everyone should have the right to earn a decent living, one that supports an individual, as well as his or her family. This isn't always the case, however. We know that the unemployment rate in many countries is disheartening. We need to strive to make sure that everyone is able to have a well-deserved standard of living. It is part of our call to stewardship.

Side Note
Anyone who does not do an honest day's work for an honest day's pay is, in fact, stealing from his or her employer.

Many companies are investigated for withholding employees' overtime pay, benefits, or other wages. Such actions violate the seventh commandment and are a social injustice.

Those who have the most are called to share with those who are less fortunate. This example may help explain our world's food distribution: Ten members of a family sit down to eat one large pizza. The pizza is cut in ten equal pieces. The three oldest members proceed to take eight and one-half pieces. That leaves just one and one-half pieces to be shared among the seven younger members. That is approximately how the world's food and other goods are being distributed among the world population today.

The more developed countries (28 percent of the world's population) also have over 80 percent of the world's income and wealth. Put most simply, the rich countries have the available food, land, equipment, fertilizer, labor, and other goods. The poor countries (72 percent) do not. Rather than sharing their wealth and excess goods, the more developed countries (which includes the United States) spend money on luxuries and waste food and other goods.

Catechism Clip
God blesses those who come to the aid of the poor and rebukes those who turn away from them. . . . (#2443)

Love for those who are poor

It has always been a tradition of the Catholic Church to care for and to love those who are poor. This love is inspired by Jesus' concern for those who are poor and his own poverty. It is by what we have done for the poverty-stricken that Jesus Christ will recognize his chosen ones. When her mother reproached her for caring for those who were poor and sick at home, Saint Rose of Lima said to her, "When we serve the poor and the sick, we serve Jesus. We must not fail to help our neighbors, because in them we serve Jesus."

The *works of mercy* are charitable actions by which we come to the aid of our neighbor for both spiritual and bodily necessities. Instructing, advising, consoling, and comforting are the Spiritual Works of Mercy, as are forgiving and bearing wrongs patiently. The Corporal Works of Mercy consist especially in feeding the hungry, sheltering the homeless, clothing the naked, visiting the sick and imprisoned, and burying the dead. Among all these, giving alms to those who are poor is one of the chief witnesses to communal charity; it is also a work of justice pleasing to God.

WORKS OF MERCY

Christians are given two guides for how we should treat and help the people in the world. The first list, the Corporal Works of Mercy, guides us in helping fulfill our neighbors' most basic bodily needs.

1. Feed the hungry.
2. Give drink to the thirsty.
3. Clothe the naked.
4. Visit the imprisoned.
5. Shelter the homeless.
6. Visit the sick.
7. Bury the dead.

The second list, the Spiritual Works of Mercy, draws our attention to the spiritual needs of people.

1. Counsel the doubtful.
2. Instruct the ignorant.
3. Admonish the sinner.
4. Comfort the sorrowful.
5. Forgive injuries.
6. Bear wrongs patiently.
7. Pray for the living and the dead.

Journal

Describe one time when you performed one of the Corporal Works of Mercy.

How did you feel?

Describe one time when you performed one of the Spiritual Works of Mercy.

How did you feel?

Why is it important to perform these works of mercy?

Now describe one time when someone performed one of the Corporal Works of Mercy for you.

How did you feel?

Now describe one time when someone performed one of the Spiritual Works of Mercy for you.

How did you feel?

CHARITY BALL

Separate into groups of four. Once you are in your group, take a closer look at the Corporal and Spiritual Works of Mercy. Each person should then choose one person they know who practices these works. It may be someone famous, a leader from your community, or one of your relatives. Assume that these four people have been invited to a charity ball honoring them for their works of mercy. Put together a short skit showing how the four people might interact. Be sure to relate to your audience how each person acts out the works of mercy.

Scripture Search

Read 2 Samuel 12:1–4. What is wrong with the actions of the rich man? Why? How does this apply to the tenth commandment?

CAN YOU DO BETTER?

Separate into groups of four. You will need a pencil or pen, a sheet of paper, a scissors, and a large round object, such as a coffee can or lid. Trace the can or lid onto the paper; then separate the circle into ten equal sections. Cut the sections apart. If there are four of you in the group, how can you divide up the ten pieces so that each of you has an equal amount? Note any creative strategies that you need to use. Once you have completed this activity, discuss your group's strategy with your classmates. Did you all use the same method? Why or why not? What did you learn about problem solving and justice?

THE BEATITUDES IN ACTION

Separate into five groups. Each group should be assigned one of the Scripture passages below. As a group, read the passage aloud. Discuss what it means, as well as how it relates to the seventh and tenth commandments. Take what you have learned from your passage and apply it to your everyday life, in a way that is relevant to you today. As a group, write a short story incorporating the lesson from the Beatitudes in a current-day situation.

- Matthew 6:1–4
- Matthew 6:16–18
- Matthew 6:19–21
- Matthew 7:1–6
- Matthew 6:25–34

Take turns reading your short stories to the class.

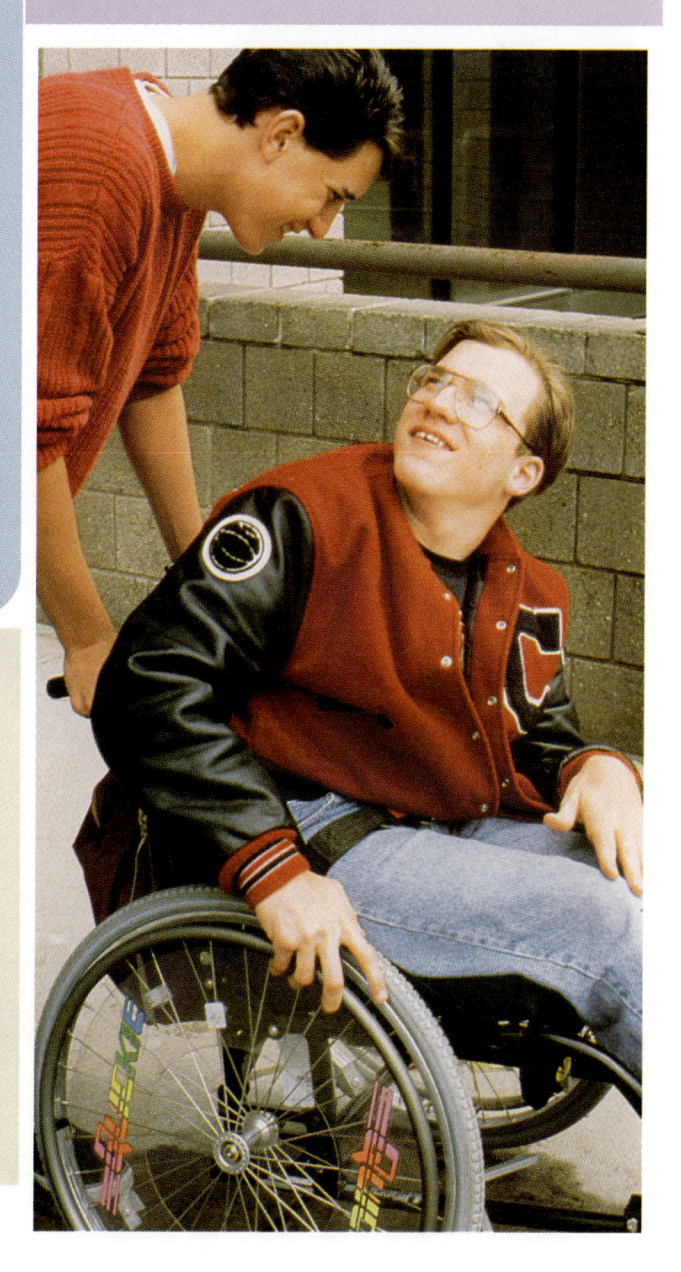

Reparation

Sometimes we take our eyes off the goal of true happiness and fail to follow the seventh or tenth commandments. When you have wronged another person, it is important to make reparation for what you have done. To make *reparation* means to make up with, or to pay back, the person you have hurt. When we sin, we ask the Lord for forgiveness. It is also important to ask the person you have hurt for forgiveness and to mend any hurt feelings between you. As the *Catechism* tells us:

> *Jesus blesses Zacchaeus for his pledge: "If I have defrauded anyone of anything, I restore it fourfold." [Lk 19:8.] Those who, directly or indirectly, have taken possession of the goods of another, are obliged to make restitution of them, or to return the equivalent in kind or in money, if the goods have disappeared, as well as the profit or advantages their owner would have legitimately obtained from them. Likewise, all who in some manner have taken part in a theft or who have knowingly benefited from it—for example, those who ordered it, assisted in it, or received the stolen goods—are obliged to make restitution in proportion to their responsibility and to their share of what was stolen. (#2412)*

Scripture Search

Silently read the story of the rich young man in Luke 18:18–25.

How difficult would it be for you to give up your worldly possessions to obtain eternal life?

What would be the most difficult possession to give up?

If you were the rich young man in the story, how would you have responded to Jesus' words?

Pause to Pray

Jesus, your heart went out to the rich young man.

You loved his earnestness and understood his struggles.

You also recognized and were saddened by the paralyzing power that possessions held over him.

Liberate any rich persons who are in bondage to their wealth.

Help them achieve the liberty of spirit that is beyond price so that they may be unrestrained in their generosity.

Let them experience their solidarity with those who are poor and suffering so that they may experience more deeply your love and your peace.

Touch our own hearts so we will not be blinded by the wealth of others into undervaluing their generosity or judging them too severely.

To the extent that any of us are rich, or seem rich to others, look on us as you looked on that rich young man and free us from the bondage of possessions.

Give us open and responsive hearts that we may generously share what we have gratefully received.

Help us and all humankind to recognize and celebrate our oneness as your children united in your Spirit of peace. Amen.

—adapted from *The Fire of Peace,* written by **Jim Dinn**

Journal

Have you ever stolen anything? If so, what? What were the consequences? What did you learn from the experience?

_____
_____
_____
_____

What are some things that you, personally, can do to express your stewardship?

_____
_____
_____
_____

Homework

1. Look back at your homework from chapter 1. You were to read each of the Ten Commandments, and then put each commandment into your own words. How did you phrase the seventh and tenth commandments? Now that you have completed chapter 7, is there anything that you would like to add? Take this time to record any changes here in your textbook.

2. Before the next class period, "let a walk take you." Step out, by yourself, with no particular destination in mind. Just walk. As you walk, take note of everything around you: the sights, the sounds, the smells. Immediately after your walk, write down some of the things that you noticed.

Sights

Sounds

Smells

Feelings

Thoughts

- What surprised you about your walk?

- What did you notice in regard to the careful or reckless use of resources?

- How did your walk relate to the seventh and tenth commandments?

- How would you describe the overall experience?

Chapter 8
You Shall Not Bear False Witness

TO TELL THE TRUTH

Separate the class into two groups. Designate one half of the room Team A, the other half Team B. As a team, take a few minutes to brainstorm a list of statements about the members of your group. Some should be true, and some should be false. As teams, take turns reciting your statements to the other team. Everyone should get a turn. After each statement, pause and ask the other team, "True or False"? Each time that the other team guesses correctly as to which statements are true and which are false, they get one point. After playing, answer these questions:

- Was it easy or difficult to tell which statements were true and which were false?

- Did any one of the other team's gestures or voice inflections give you a clue? If so, what?

The source of all truth

You have most likely heard the phrase, "If you can't say anything nice, then don't say anything at all." This is at the heart of the eighth commandment. So is truth. Truth is fact or reality. It is accurate information.

The eighth commandment—*"You shall not bear false witness against your neighbor"* (Exodus 20:16)—upholds a very basic principle: we all have a right to the truth or knowledge we need for living and growing and caring for ourselves. You violate this commandment, then, whenever you deliberately give others false information to mislead them or prevent them from knowing the truth that they have a right to know.

Lying is clearly a violation of this commandment, and it occurs in a variety of forms. False advertisements, false rumors, false promises, and false witness are all different kinds of lies. There are libel (lying in print) and slander (lying verbally). Just as there are many types of lies, there are many reasons for lying. In this chapter, we will take a closer look at what lying is, what it does, and why people do it.

It is not always easy to tell what is true and what is false. The important thing is to make sure that you tell the truth so that others, God, and yourself will know you as a true and honest individual.

As human beings, we have a tendency to tell the truth. Remember when you were younger, and you couldn't wait to tell your parents what your brother or sister had done while they had been away? Part of the reason for that is because we *want* to tell the truth. If we want to tell the truth, then why don't we always do it?

Journal

Describe a time that you lied. What was your reason for lying? How did you feel about yourself?

Why people lie

One of the reasons that people lie is to avoid some punishment for a wrong action. For example, you might make up some excuse about why you don't have your homework done so that your teacher won't punish you and lower your grade (which in turn could cause your parents to punish you as well). You may lie about where you were, what you were doing, or who you were with so that your parents won't ground you. Avoiding having to take responsibility for a wrong action is one reason that people lie—and it is perhaps the most common one.

Often people lie to avoid an unpleasant task or situation. You don't want to go to school, so you pretend that you are ill. You might want to watch TV rather than do homework, so you tell your mom that you don't have any homework tonight, or you say that you've already finished it. This, too, is a common reason why people lie.

Another reason that people lie is to get something that they want, such as more money, certain friends, or special treatment. This is the motive behind most false advertising and lying in business. A used car salesman may lie about the quality of a car to make a sale. A person may lie on a job application form, saying that he or she has experience that he or she doesn't have. Some people even make fake "handicapped" signs in their cars so that they can park in a handicapped spot! This is also why people cheat on tests—to get grades that they haven't truly earned.

Sometimes people lie to be popular, to impress others, or to get people to like and respect them. Young people may make up stories of sexual prowess to impress their friends. Politicians have a reputation for this kind of lying in order to gain respect, especially during campaign speeches. This kind of lying may sometimes contain a grain of truth. A person did catch a fish, but then "stretches" the truth about how big it actually was. Even if the person is bragging or boasting, it is still lying.

Scripture Search

Read 1 Peter 2:1–6. To what situation does Peter compare people who are striving to be honest in their words and actions?

WHERE DO YOU SEE IT?

We see these types of lies all over the place, don't we? One of the most common places that we see lying is on TV. Have you ever been watching a sitcom and thought to yourself, "No, don't lie. You'll only mess things up worse!"? It can be uncomfortable to watch, yet sometimes we do the same things in our own lives.

In small groups, brainstorm as many TV episodes of different shows that you can think of that involved lying. List the TV show, a brief description of the episode, and a way that conflict could have been avoided without lying.

TV show   **Brief description**   **Way conflict could have been avoided**

Called to bear witness

Have you ever overheard someone saying bad things about another person that you knew? If so, what did you do? As Christians, we are called to bear witness to the truth, and to stand up for ourselves and for others. Sometimes we have to stand up for the truth even when it isn't "cool." One saying reads, "Stand up for what is right, even if you're standing alone."

We are called to be witnesses of the gospel, which means that we have an obligation to be Christ-like. Let's say that a friend approaches you with a rumor about one of your classmates. The temptation is to pass on the rumor. The Christ-like thing to do, however, is to avoid repeating what you have heard or to walk away from hearing it altogether.

A *martyr* is someone who gives supreme witness to his or her faith. A martyr gives his or her life for God, just as Christ did. Just because you don't have to give up your life doesn't mean you are not called to be a witness of the gospel. It is important to note, however, that many people have paid this ultimate cost so that we might have the faith that we have today.

JUST THE FACTS

Separate into small groups. With your partners, research someone who has been a martyr for his or her faith. Once you have selected someone, complete the following information:

Who we selected:

Why:

When this person lived:

Where:

Why he or she died for his or her faith:

What we learned:

Once you have completed this information, plus any additional facts that you may want to include, prepare a presentation for your class. Perhaps you want to present your material as a made-for-TV movie or as a cartoon. Be as creative as you wish—but remember to stick to the facts!

Scripture Search

Read the following excerpt from Saint Paul's letter to the Ephesians (4:25–32). What are three of the main points that Paul is stressing?

1.
2.
3.

Now write a short speech of your own that stresses these three points. Give specific examples of how to live these ideas in real life. Present your speech to the class.

What's in a lie?

There are many ways in which people commit offenses against the truth. All of them are offenses of the eighth commandment. It is important to avoid these so that we can live as Jesus did.

- A statement in court that is contrary to the truth is known as *false witness*.
- A false statement under oath is called *perjury*.
- *Adulation* is to flatter or admire excessively.
- *Boasting* or *bragging* is to portray one's self as more than what one truly is.

TO DEFAME THE FAMOUS

Actors and actresses often sue magazines and newspapers for purposely printing incorrect and harmful information about them. This is called *libel*. It means using written or printed words, pictures, and so forth, to defame, or to attack the reputation, of others.

Your teacher has several examples of media publications that are often known to contain false information. Look through the magazines and newspapers and locate information that you believe would be harmful to the reputations of the actors or actresses. Share your examples and reasoning with the class.

Chances are you may not be asked to be a witness at a trial in the near future, or for that matter, ever. Any time that you deliberately keep others from the truth that they need to know, however, it's lying, and you are involved in a kind of false witness. Suppose that your mom or dad asks, "Where are you going?" or "With whom are you going?" As your parents, they have the right to know this kind of information so that they can fulfill their responsibility to guide and to protect you. Your answer may be vague or only partially true. You might say, "We're going to the park," but fail to add, "And then we're going to an R-rated movie." You may make up a total lie. No matter how you do it, if you deliberately mislead or prevent your parents from knowing the real truth by what you say—or by what you don't say—then it's false witness or lying.

Side Note

An increasing number of schools across the United States are developing harassment policies. Under these policies, a student and his or her parents could be sued if the student is responsible for harming the reputation of another student through his or her words or actions.

This obligation to truthfully share the information others have a right to know applies to every relationship in your life, not just to the relationships with your parents and family. It applies to teachers, friends, classmates, and even strangers. Lying is lying, regardless of how you mislead others and regardless of who the others are.

WHO ARE "OTHERS"?

Below, list as many people as you can think of with whom you need to be honest and truthful. Then list some ways in which you can be certain to maintain their trust.

• People with whom I need to be honest and truthful:

• Ways in which I can be certain to maintain their trust:

93

When a lie occurs

When a person lies, the gravity, or seriousness, must be taken into consideration. This is measured against:

- The nature of the truth it distorts;
- The circumstances;
- The intentions of the one who is lying; and
- The harm suffered by victims of the lie.

Any kind of lying is wrong, but some lies can put people in danger. For example, let's say that you know that your friend walked off with someone that he or she didn't know, and your friend hasn't returned for some time. Your friend's mom calls and asks if you've seen her, and you say that you don't know where your friend is. You think that your lie is protecting your friend because you know that her mom would be mad if she went off with a stranger, but in fact your lie could be putting your friend in danger. If your friend doesn't know the person, she could be in danger, and you have an obligation to tell the truth.

It's only right

Just as you need to make reparation for theft, you need to make reparation when you commit an offense against someone's reputation since it is an offense against the truth. Let your conscience guide you, and make reparation in relation to the damage caused.

If you have spread a rumor about one of your classmates, approach him or her, confess to what you have done, and ask for forgiveness. It would also be a good idea to tell your classmates about your false information. Something that seems harmless enough can cause another person a great deal of stress and sadness, and you do not have the right to do that to another human being. What we do to each other we in turn do to God.

Journal
Has anyone ever lied or started a rumor about you? How did you feel? How did you react?
___
___
___

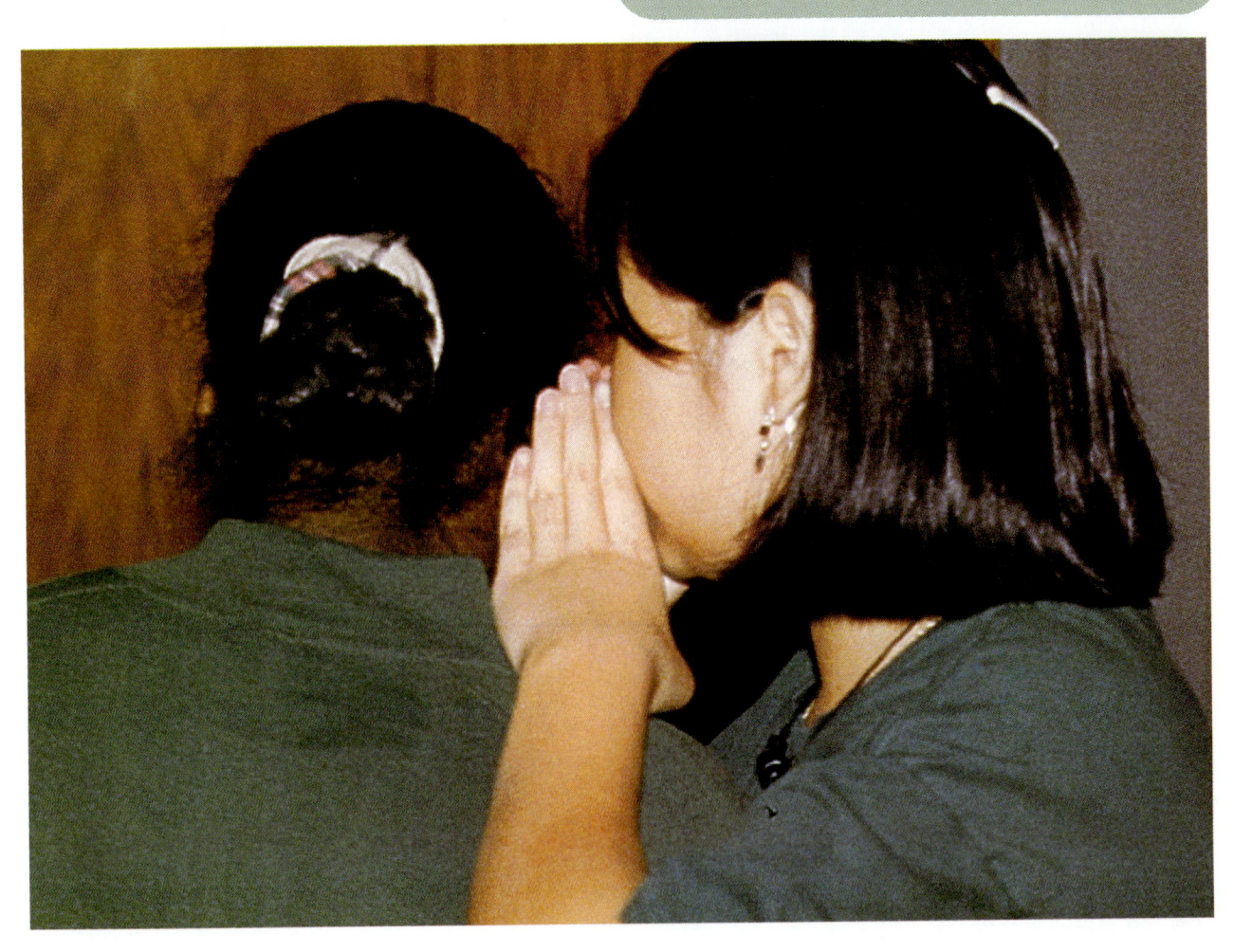

Scripture Search

As a class, read together James 3:1–12. What images does this passage create? What is the passage's strongest message?

ACTIONS SPEAK LOUDER THAN WORDS

Separate the class into four small groups. Each group should prepare a skit of a situation in which someone lies. After each skit is acted out for the class, the group should say "Take Two!" and follow with a skit of the same situation in which the person makes a more honest choice.

The Golden Rule

If we just remember to follow the Golden Rule and do unto others as we would have them do unto us, then we can avoid a lot of sticky situations in life. We all have a right to the truth, and we should be careful not to infringe upon the rights of others.

All you need to know

As was stated in chapter 1, the Ten Commandments express our fundamental duties toward God and toward our neighbor—to love God and to love one another. They describe the basic moral law for being fully human and fully happy. The Ten Commandments are engraved by God in the human heart.

Like the Golden Rule and the Beatitudes, all ten of the commandments are an extension of love: love for God, love for family (the domestic church), love for self, and love for neighbor. Following the commandments is a way of showing your respect for God.

LIVING WHAT YOU'VE LEARNED

In small groups, list one specific example of how you are to live each of the commandments. You can do this by writing what you are to do or by writing what you are not to do.

- "I am the Lord your God; you shall not have strange gods before me."

- "You shall not take the name of the Lord your God in vain."

- "Remember to keep holy the Sabbath day."

- "Honor your father and mother."

- "You shall not kill."

- "You shall not commit adultery."

- "You shall not steal."

- "You shall not bear false witness."

- "You shall not covet your neighbor's wife."

- "You shall not covet your neighbor's goods."

Scripture Search

Once more, read the Decalogue: Exodus 20:2–17. Which commandment do you need to follow more closely in your life? Why?

Which commandment do you feel is the most difficult to follow? Why?

If you could add one more commandment that you feel our world needs today, what would you add?

Pause to Pray

Dear Lord,
Help me be mindful of my words and my actions.
Give me the courage to speak honestly and act justly.
I want to be someone who acts as Jesus did.
I now have a better understanding of what that means,
and I pray that I will go forth from this class with renewed vision.
May others know that I am a Christian by my love and by my honesty.
I ask this through Christ our Lord. Amen.

Journal

In what way is your attitude toward the Ten Commandments now different from when you first began this course?

What is the most important *new* thing that you learned from this course?

Homework

1. Look back at your homework from chapter 1. You were to read each of the Ten Commandments, then put each commandment into your own words. How did you phrase the eighth commandment? Now that you have completed chapter 8, is there anything that you would like to add? Take time to record any changes.

2. Imagine that you meet a person who has never heard of the Ten Commandments. How would you explain to that person the real nature of the commandments and why they are important to know and follow? In the space provided, write a dialogue explaining what you would tell this person. If time permits, ask a classmate to read aloud with you the dialogue you have written.

Appendix I: Glossary of Terms

adulation: to flatter or admire excessively

adultery: when a married person voluntarily takes part in sexual relations and/or intercourse with someone other than his or her lawful spouse

avarice: a disordered thirst for riches

blasphemy: to show irreverence or disrespect for God or for sacred images

boasting (bragging): to portray one's self as more than what one truly is

carte blanche: the ability to do whatever you want with little or no regard of others

charity: to love God above all things for God's own sake and to love our neighbors as ourselves for the love of God

chastity: the state or quality of remaining chaste, meaning that you refrain from taking part in unlawful (or nonmarital) sexual intercourse

commandment: a divine law, a direction from God

covenant: a pact, an agreement, a contract, or a set of mutual promises

covenant people: the parties involved in a set of mutual promises

covet: to wrongfully desire what someone else has

Decalogue: another word for the Ten Commandments, meaning ten words

domestic church: another name for a family, a community based on faith, hope, and love

euthanasia: the act or practice of killing or permitting the death of hopelessly sick or injured individuals in a relatively painless way for reasons of mercy

faith: to believe in the one and only true God and to believe in God's love for you

false witness: a statement in court that is contrary to the truth

filial piety: the respect that children have for their parents or guardians

fornication: the sexual union between an unmarried man and an unmarried woman

guides: people who help us become the best people we can be

grace: God's free gift of himself, the offer of God's love to humanity, which precedes our yearning for God and our free response

hope: to trust in God above all else and in God's promise always to love, care for, and when necessary, forgive you

justice: preserving and respecting the rights of others and giving them what they deserve (fair treatment of all people)

lust: a strong, disordered desire for another human being

martyr: someone who gives supreme witness to his or her faith

masturbation: the deliberate stimulation of the sexual organs in order to achieve sexual pleasure

moral law: a law written to describe how people need to treat each other and relate in order to survive and to be happy together

natural law: the inborn sense that knows the difference between right and wrong

natural moral law: the original moral sense within all people that calls them to use reason to choose good and to avoid evil

oath: a solemn vow to God that you will speak the truth or keep a promise

parish: a definite community within a particular church under the pastoral care of a priest

perjury: a false statement under oath

physical law: a law dictated by nature, describing the facts about how things are, how they work, and how they relate to each other

polytheism: the belief and worship of more than one god

pornography: highly-sexual materials that are considered evil because they remove sexual acts from the intimacy of the partners involved

presumption: a sin against hope that manifests itself in two ways: when a person hopes he or she can save himself or herself without help from God and when a person hopes he or she can obtain forgiveness without conversion and glory without merit

prostitution: reducing a person to an instrument of sexual pleasure or money

rape: forcing sexual intimacy onto another person

solidarity: obeying the Golden Rule of doing unto others what you would like done unto you, especially for those who are poor

temperance: moderation that requires us to control and to limit our attachment to worldly goods and pleasures

venerate: to show respect for something, such as a sacred image

Appendix II: Your Catholic Heritage
TRADITIONAL PRAYERS

Sign of the Cross

In the name of the Father,
and of the Son,
and of the Holy Spirit.
Amen.

The Lord's Prayer

Our Father, who art in heaven,
hallowed be your name;
your kingdom come;
your will be done on earth
as it is in heaven.
Give us this day our daily bread;
and forgive us our trespasses
as we forgive those
who trespass against us;
and lead us not into temptation,
but deliver us from evil. Amen.

Hail Mary

Hail, Mary, full of grace,
the Lord is with you!
Blessed are you among women,
and blessed is the fruit of your womb, Jesus.
Holy Mary, Mother of God,
pray for us sinners,
now and at the hour of our death.
Amen.

Trinity Prayer

Glory to the Father,
and to the Son,
and to the Holy Spirit.
As it was in the beginning, is now,
and will be forever. Amen.

La Señal de la Cruz

Por la señal de la Santz Cruz,
de nuestros enemigos libranos,
Señor, Dios nuestro.
En el nombre del Padre
y del Hijo
y del Espíritu Santo. Amén.

El Padre Nuestro

Padre nuestro, que estás en el cielo,
santificado sea tu nombre,
Venga a nosotros tu reino;
hágase tu voluntad en la tierra
como en el cielo.
Danos hoy nuestro pan de cade día;
perdona nuestras ofensas,
como también nosotros perdonamos
a los que nos ofenden,
No nos dejes caer en tentación,
y líbranos del mal. Amén.

El Ave María

Dios te salve, María, llena eres de gracia,
el Señor es contigo.
Bendita tú eres entre todas las mujeres,
y bendito es el fruto de tu vientre, Jesús.
Santa María, Madre de Dios,
ruega por nosotros pecadores,
ahora, y en la hora de nuestra muerte.
Amén.

La Oración a La Trinidad

Gloria al Padre, al Hijo, y al Espíritu Santo;
como era en el principio, ahora, y siempre,
por los siglos de los siglos. Amén.

OTHER PRAYERS

Blessing Before Meals

Bless us, O Lord, and these your gifts
which we are about to receive from your
goodness, through Christ our Lord. Amen.

Thanksgiving After Meals

We give you thanks for all your gifts, Almighty
God, living and reigning now and forever. Amen.

Act of Contrition

O my God, I am sorry for my sins.
In choosing to sin and failing to do good,
I have sinned against you
and your Church.
I firmly intend, with the help of your Son,
to do penance and to sin no more. Amen.

I Confess

I confess to almighty God,
and to you, my brothers and sisters
that I have sinned through my own fault
in my thoughts and in my words,
in what I have done,
and in what I have failed to do;
and I ask blessed Mary, ever virgin,
all the angels and saints,
and you, my brothers and sisters,
to pray for me to the Lord our God.

Prayer to the Holy Spirit

Come, Holy Spirit, fill the hearts of your faithful,
And kindle in them the fire of your love.
Send forth your Spirit and they shall be created.
And you shall renew the face of the earth.
Lord, by the light of the Holy Spirit
you have taught the hearts of your faithful.
In the same Spirit
help us relish what is right
and always rejoice in your consolation.
We ask this through Christ our Lord. Amen.

Prayer of St. Alphonsus Liguori

Grant me the gift of knowledge, so I may know the
things of God and, enlightened by your holy
teaching, may walk without deviation in the path of
eternal salvation.

Serenity Prayer

O God, grant me the serenity
to accept the things I cannot change,
the courage to change the things I can,
and the wisdom to know the difference.
Amen.

The Jesus Prayer

Lord Jesus Christ,
Son of God,
have mercy on me, a sinner.
Amen.

RULES CATHOLICS LIVE BY

The Great Commandments

"Love the Lord your God
with all your heart
with all your soul
with all your strength, and
with all your mind;
love your neighbor as you love yourself."
(Luke 10:27; Deuteronomy 6:5; Leviticus 19:18)

Jesus' Law of Love

"Love one another as I have loved you." (John 15:12)

The Ten Commandments

1. I am the LORD your God. You shall not have strange gods before me.
2. You shall not take the name of the LORD your God in vain.
3. Remember to keep holy the LORD's day.
4. Honor your father and your mother.
5. You shall not kill.
6. You shall not commit adultery.
7. You shall not steal.
8. You shall not bear false witness against your neighbor.
9. You shall not covet your neighbor's wife.
10. You shall not covet your neighbor's goods.

Precepts of the Church

1. You shall attend Mass on Sundays and on holy days of obligation and rest from servile labor.
2. You shall confess your sins at least once a year.
3. You shall receive the Sacrament of the Eucharist at least during the Easter Season.
4. You shall observe the days of fasting and abstinence established by the Church.
5. You shall help provide for the needs of the Church.

WHAT CATHOLICS BELIEVE

Nicene Creed

We believe in one God,
the Father, the Almighty,
maker of heaven and earth,
of all that is seen and unseen.
We believe in one Lord, Jesus Christ,
the only Son of God,
eternally begotten of the Father,
God from God, Light from Light,
true God from true God,
begotten, not made, one in Being with the Father.
Through him all things were made.
For us men and for our salvation
he came down from heaven:
by the power of the Holy Spirit
he was born of the Virgin Mary, and became man.
For our sake he was crucified under Pontius Pilate;
he suffered, died, and was buried.
On the third day he rose again
in fulfillment of the Scriptures;
he ascended into heaven
and is seated at the right hand of the Father.
He will come again in glory
    to judge the living and the dead,
and his kingdom will have no end.
We believe in the Holy Spirit, the Lord, the giver of life,
who proceeds from the Father and the Son.
With the Father and the Son he is worshiped and glorified.
He has spoken through the prophets.
We believe in one holy catholic and apostolic Church.
We acknowledge one baptism for the forgiveness of sins.
We look for the resurrection of the dead,
and the life of the world to come. Amen.

Eucharistic Prayer IV

Father, we acknowledge your greatness:
all your actions show your wisdom and love.
You formed man in your own likeness
and set him over the whole world
to serve you, his creator,
and to rule over all creatures.
Even when he disobeyed you and lost your friendship,
you did not abandon him to the power of death,
but helped all men to seek and find you.
Again and again you offered a covenant to man,
and through the prophets taught him to hope for salvation.
Father, you so loved the world
that in the fullness of time you sent
your only Son to be our Savior.
He was conceived through the power of the Holy Spirit,
and born of the Virgin Mary,
a man like us in all things but sin.
To the poor he proclaimed the good news of salvation,
to prisoners, freedom,
and to those in sorrow, joy.
In fulfillment of your will
he gave himself up to death;
but by rising from the dead,
he destroyed death and restored life.
And that we might live no longer for ourselves but for him,
he sent the Holy Spirit from you, Father,
as his first gift to those who believe,
to complete his work on earth
and bring us the fullness of grace.

Father, may this Holy Spirit sanctify these offerings.

Let them become the body and blood of Jesus Christ our Lord

as we celebrate the great mystery

which he left us as an everlasting covenant.

He always loved those who were his own in the world.

When the time came for him to be glorified by you, his heavenly Father,

he showed the depth of his love.

While they were at supper,

he took bread, said the blessing, broke the bread,

and gave it to his disciples, saying:

Take this, all of you, and eat it:

this is my body which will be given up for you.

In the same way, he took the cup, filled with wine.

He gave you thanks, and giving the cup to his disciples, said:

Take this all of you and drink from it:

this is the cup of my blood,

the blood of the new and everlasting covenant.

It will be shed for you and for all

so that sins may be forgiven.

Do this in memory of me.

Let us proclaim the mystery of faith:

A Christ has died,

   Christ is risen,

   Christ will come again.

B Dying you destroyed our death

   rising you restored our life.

   Lord Jesus, come in glory.

C When we eat this bread and drink this cup,

   we proclaim your death, Lord Jesus,

   until you come in glory.

D Lord, by your cross and resurrection

   you have set us free.

   You are the Savior of the world.

Father, we now celebrate this memorial of our redemption.

We recall Christ's death, his descent among the dead,

his resurrection and ascension to your right hand;

and, looking forward to his coming in glory,

we offer you his body and blood,

the acceptable sacrifice

which brings salvation to the whole world.

Lord, look upon this sacrifice which you have given to your Church;

and by your Holy Spirit, gather all who share this one bread and one cup

into the one body of Christ, a living sacrifice of praise.

Lord, remember those for whom we offer this sacrifice,

especially N. our Pope,

N. our bishop, and bishops and clergy everywhere.

Remember those who take part in this offering,

those here present and all your people,

and all who seek you with a sincere heart.

Remember those who have died in the peace of Christ

and all the dead whose faith is known to you alone.

Father, in your mercy grant also to us, your children,

to enter into our heavenly inheritance

in the company of the Virgin Mary, the Mother of God,

and your apostles and saints.

Then, in your kingdom, freed from the corruption of sin and death,

we shall sing your glory with every creature through Christ our Lord,

through whom you give us everything that is good.

Through him,

with him,

in him,

in the unity of the Holy Spirit,

all glory and honor is yours,

Almighty Father,

forever and ever.

Amen.

Gifts of the Holy Spirit

Wisdom

Understanding

Right judgment (Counsel)

Courage (Fortitude)

Knowledge

Reverence (Piety)

Wonder and Awe (Fear of the Lord)

Fruits of the Spirit

Charity	Generosity
Joy	Gentleness
Peace	Faithfulness
Patience	Modesty
Kindness	Self-control
Goodness	Chastity

Theological Virtues

Faith

Hope

Love

Cardinal Virtues

Prudence

Justice

Fortitude

Temperence

Works of Mercy

Corporal (for the body)

Feed the hungry.

Give drink to the thirsty.

Clothe the naked.

Shelter the homeless.

Visit the sick.

Visit the imprisoned.

Bury the dead.

Spiritual (for the spirit)

Warn the sinner.

Teach the ignorant.

Counsel the doubtful.

Comfort the sorrowful.

Bear wrongs patiently.

Forgive injuries.

Pray for the living and the dead.

CATHOLIC DEVOTIONS AND PRACTICES

The Rosary

The Joyful Mysteries

(Mondays and Thursdays)

1. The annunciation
2. The visitation
3. The birth of Jesus
4. The presentation in the Temple
5. Mary and Joseph find Jesus in the Temple

The Sorrowful Mysteries

(Tuesdays and Fridays)

1. The agony in the garden
2. The scourging of Jesus
3. The crowning with thorns
4. Jesus carries his cross
5. Jesus dies on the cross

The Glorious Mysteries

(Sundays, Wednesdays, and Saturdays)

1. The resurrection
2. The ascension
3. The Holy Spirit is sent upon the apostles
4. The assumption of Mary
5. Mary is crowned queen of heaven and earth

Stations of the Cross

Traditional

1. Jesus is condemned to death.
2. Jesus takes up his cross.
3. Jesus falls the first time.
4. Jesus meets his sorrowful mother.
5. Simon of Cyrene helps Jesus.
6. Veronica wipes the face of Jesus.
7. Jesus falls a second time.
8. Jesus meets the women of Jerusalem.
9. Jesus falls a third time.
10. Jesus is stripped of his clothing.
11. Jesus is nailed to the cross.
12. Jesus dies on the cross.
13. Jesus' body is removed from the cross.
14. Jesus' body is placed in the tomb.

Scriptural

1. Jesus prays in the Garden of Olives.
2. Jesus is betrayed by Judas and arrested.
3. Jesus is condemned by the Sanhedrin.
4. Jesus is denied by Peter.
5. Jesus is condemned by Pontius Pilate.
6. Jesus is scourged and crowned with thorns.
7. Jesus is made to carry the cross.
8. Simon of Cyrene helps Jesus.
9. Jesus meets the women of Jerusalem.
10. Jesus is crucified.
11. Jesus promises the kingdom to the thief who repents.
12. Jesus speaks to his mother and his friend John.
13. Jesus dies on the cross.
14. Jesus is laid in the tomb.

Prayer for the Way of the Cross

We adore you, O Christ, and we bless you,
because by your holy cross
you have redeemed the world.

Holy Days in the United States

Christmas, the Birth of Jesus—December 25

Solemnity of Mary, Mother of God—January 1

Ascension of the Lord—the fortieth day (Thursday) after Easter

Assumption of Mary into Heaven—August 15

All Saints' Day—November 1

Immaculate Conception of Mary—December 8

Days of Abstinence

(Days when Catholics age 14 and over do not eat meat)

Ash Wednesday

Fridays in Lent

Good Friday

Days of Fasting

(Days when Catholics ages 18–59 eat one full meal and two smaller meals)

Ash Wednesday

Good Friday

The Sacraments

Sacraments of Initiation

Baptism

Confirmation

Eucharist

Sacraments of Healing

Reconciliation

Anointing of the Sick

Sacraments of Vocation and Service

Matrimony

Holy Orders

The Beatitudes

Blessed are the poor in spirit,
   for theirs is the kingdom of heaven.
Blessed are they who mourn,
   for they will be comforted.
Blessed are the meek,
   for they shall inherit the land.
Blessed are they who hunger and thirst for righteousness,
   for they will be satisfied.
Blessed are the merciful,
   for they will be shown mercy.
Blessed are the clean of heart,
   for they will see God.
Blessed are the peacemakers,
   for they will be called children of God.
Blessed are they who are persecuted for the sake of righteousness,
   for theirs is the kingdom of heaven.